"This book is **brilliant**. Th[...] [...]e book but the stories themselves are gems. Here is a passiona[...] [...] which have the power to shape and change lives. How can we no[...]"

– **Rt Revd John Pritchard, Bishop of Oxford and Chair of the Church of England's National Board of Education**

"This **excellent** volume of stories will enthral any child who hears them. I also hope people will resist the temptation to skip to the stories and read the sections on how to tell a story, as they are an excellent guide to what is to follow."

– **Sam Donoghue, Children's Ministry Adviser for the Diocese of London and co-editor of** *Childrenswork* **magazine**

"I will never forget the first time I heard Mark speak. He told a story that had me spellbound. *Hanging on Every Word* is not just theory but reflects a lifestyle of world-impacting generational ministry. I cannot recommend this **invaluable** resource highly enough!"

– **Andrew Shepherd, Executive Kids Minister, Edge Church International, Adelaide, Australia**

"This is an excellent resource; at turns **gripping**, moving, challenging, and inspiring. Written with a scholar's mind and a child's heart, this collection of stories is a 'must have' addition to the bookshelf of every school assembly co-ordinator."

– **Anne Davey, Director of Education, Oxford Diocese**

"Mark is a very gifted and charismatic storyteller. We all look forward to his assemblies, children and adults alike, as he brings his stories to life and mesmerises us all with his performance. I am **delighted** to endorse this book as I know the author can not only 'talk the talk' but also 'walk the walk'. I'd recommend this to anyone who delivers assemblies: the stories all have a message without seeming to preach and as Mark says… GREAT STORIES DON'T NEED TO BE EXPLAINED!"

– **Trisha Donkin, Headteacher, Holly Spring Junior School, Bracknell**

"Mark gives the novice and the seasoned storyteller a **fresh**, concise guide on how to weave and spin tales and how to captivate your audience and sweep them along with you. This book deserves to be read, told, and heard. An essential resource."

– **Jim Bailey, International children's worker and singer/songwriter**

"Mark is a **master** storyteller. This book serves up a feast of stories, along with some top-class storytelling tips so that anyone can retell them. Mark demonstrates the power of stories which speak direct to the heart. I was moved and inspired in reading them and know that these stories will have the same effect on others for years to come, shaping their future for the better. Enjoy reading, telling, and retelling this classic collection of stories as you rediscover the power of the story to communicate the truth of the greatest story on earth."

– **Olly Goldenberg, Director of Children Can, author of** *The Josiah Generation* **and former Children's Pastor at Kensington Temple, London**

"Mark understands how stories work. He understands how kids think. And he has **years of experience** telling the one to the other."

– Bob Hartman, author of *The Lion Storyteller Bible*

"I don't know a better storyteller than Mark Griffiths. Who doesn't love a good story? They stay in your heart, bring a smile to your face or a tear to your eye. I read this book sitting on the edge of my seat, as each story captured me more and more. The first part of the book has amazing tips and advice about becoming a great storyteller. The second part is filled with great stories. I can almost see and hear Mark as I read them. For any person that loves to tell stories, this book is a **must** – a great read and resource."

– Tammy Tolman, author, speaker, and Senior Minister of Church of Christ, Sydney, Australia

"Mark has offered us access into a well-tested **treasure** trove of stories that he has used to engage the wonder of children as he talks of God. I have already worked out which ones I'll be using for school assemblies and which I'll be saving for a special, Christmas all age service or for a moment when I have an audience of grandparents, parents, and children. He has drawn on the golden oldies of Oscar Wilde and Tolstoy and on lesser known tales of the mission field and also included a few from his own child-centred imagination. Here is a series of tales that can be read, made one's own, and then retold."

– Howard Worsley, Director of Mission, Trinity College Bristol

*****

The Revd Dr Mark Griffiths is married to Rhian and they have three children, Nia, Owen, and Elliot. He has been involved in running children's events and training children's leaders both nationally and internationally for many years. He passionately believes that successful children's ministry is a major key to church growth. He is author of *Fusion, Impact, Detonate, Don't Tell Cute Stories – Change Lives*, and *One Generation from Extinction* (see details below). He is Vicar of St Michael the Archangel, Warfield, Bucks.

One Generation from Extinction
ISBN: 978-1-85424-929-6

Don't Tell Cute Stories – Change Lives!
ISBN: 978-1-85424-624-0

Fusion
ISBN: 978-1-85424-526-7

Impact
ISBN: 978-1-85424-593-9

Detonate
ISBN: 978-1-85424-679-0

HANGING ON EVERY WORD

**48 of the world's greatest stories,
retold for telling out loud**

Mark Griffiths

MONARCH
BOOKS

Oxford, UK & Grand Rapids, Michigan, USA

Published by Monarch Books
an imprint of
Lion Hudson plc
Wilkinson House, Jordan Hill Road,
Oxford OX2 8DR, England
Email: monarch@lionhudson.com
www.lionhudson.com/monarch

ISBN 978 0 85721 506 2
e-ISBN 978 0 85721 507 9

First edition 2014

Acknowledgments

The following stories are based on original stories from *The Lion Storyteller Bedtime Book* and are used by kind permission of the author, Bob Hartman: "Olle and the Troll", "Polly and the Frog", "Tortoise Brings Food".
"Elizabeth and the Aeroplane" is adapted from a sermon illustration by Tony Campolo.

A catalogue record for this book is available from the British Library

Printed and bound in the UK, February 2014, LH36

**This is dedicated to Nia, Owen, Elliot and
my fabulous wife, Rhian.**
They have, of course, heard all these stories
many times.

And to the staff team at Warfield Church.
One of the best teams on the planet –
you graciously cover my many weaknesses
and allow me to excel in my strengths.
It is a joy to journey with you all,
as together we write our own story.

Two things are needed in winter: fire and stories.

Fire to warm the body,
and stories to warm the heart.

Jewish Proverb

Contents

About this Book

This is a book of stories. It is written for anyone who tells stories; teachers, church leaders, librarians, parents. We have been telling stories since the dawn of time itself. Anthropologists tell us that storytelling is central to human existence. That it's common to every known culture.

Stories are powerful. People don't act on reality, they act based on the stories they believe about reality. Stories can also be dangerous. Nazis told stories about Jews, Serbs told stories about Croats, white supremacists told stories about black people, and as a result of those stories, millions of people died. Actions were not based on reality but on the stories that people believe about reality. Stories communicate at a deeper level. They ignore the mind and speak straight to the heart. They leave deep lingering feelings. They evoke a strong response, whether joy, anger, justice, compassion, generosity...

Political debates are won with the right story, revolutions are sparked with the right story, the most turbulent soul can be calmed with the right story. Stories can drive away fear, bring hope to the hopeless, bring joy to the despondent and stir the apathetic into life.

This is a book of stories. There are lots of ways to communicate effectively both to large crowds and to individuals, using drama, video clips, PowerPoint presentations, and so on. But this is a book of stories. And whilst I was tempted to nuance these stories with little "tips", I have resisted and allowed the story to do its own work, for these are stories that stand in their own right without the need for props. There are stories of different lengths. If you are using the talks for school assemblies, then some will fit into the assembly time slot with a song before and notices afterwards; some will fill the whole assembly slot. That's the joy of primary school assemblies, schools can be very flexible – particularly if they enjoy what you bring. However, if you are using these stories for all-age talks then you have much more freedom and can choose according to theme. And if these are stories for bedtimes, then enjoy, for you there are no time constraints.

This is a book of stories from a variety of sources. There are adaptations of stories from master storytellers of different generations: Oscar Wilde's "The Young King", "The Selfish Giant", and "The Happy Prince", and Bob Hartman's "Olle and the Troll", "Polly and the Frog", and "Tortoise Brings Food". Last but not least Tolstoy's "The Shoemaker" is a must for Christmas. Several traditional (and often neglected legends) from around the world are included, along with true-life tales of Christian world changers: Gladys Aylward, William Booth, George Muller, Jackie Pullinger, and the heart-warming story of Amy Carmichael praying for blue eyes.[1] These are combined with wondrous tales of adventure, delightful everyday stories, and several of my own original stories written to fit school assembly themes when no other stories would work. And there are many more.

What may prove surprising is there are no bible stories. Why? Well, firstly because Bob Hartman's *Lion Storyteller Bible* could not be improved on. But more than that, I have become convinced that there is a whole wealth of stories that create a sense of mystery, awe, and wonder, that communicate God without mentioning God, that present love and life and joy. After all, Jesus wasn't retelling Old Testament Bible stories when he talked of the Good Samaritan or the Foolish Builders. Jesus used stories. All stories.

1   Taken from my earlier books *Fusion, Impact* and *Detonate*, Oxford, Monarch Books.

About this Book

Modern stories are written to be read whereas ancient stories were written to be told. The stories in this book are to be told. Not read out loud – told. Some of them have been re-crafted for this purpose. It's not difficult, in fact it's incredibly natural. If you were married and I said, "Tell me about your wedding day?" or "Tell me how you proposed or were proposed to?" you wouldn't reach for your notes, you'd tell me. If I asked you to tell me about your kids you wouldn't tell me to wait until you had sorted out a PowerPoint presentation. Storytelling is just that, it is the telling of an event, the recounting of a journey.

Don't just jump into the stories. On the following pages I will share with you a few basic pointers that will transform even the most nervous person into a confident storyteller in no time.

It's a Journey

This is the key to the whole thing. It is a journey. Modern communicators have somehow got the idea that it is about communicating facts, about imparting nuggets of information. No. Creating a compelling story is about crafting an experience. It is about the joy and pain, wonder and angst, uncertainty and delight of journeying. And like any memorable journey, we are likely to be changed by it. For therein lies the crux, storytelling is transformative. At the end of the story, you are likely to be a different you to the one that started it. Stories are transformative. Not convinced? Let's try one. This is the story of John Blanchard from my book *Don't Tell Cute Stories – Change Lives*.

John Blanchard was a lieutenant in the Second World War. His hobby was reading books. I know this may not seem like the sort of thing lieutenants in the US Navy would do, but whenever he had free time John would sneak off to the library. On this particular day he had gone to the library and picked up a book bound in light blue material from the shelf. He began to read but was distracted by the comments that had been written in the margins of the book by who he guessed was the book's previous owner.

At the end of the book he found the name and address of the previous owner, one Hollis Maynell, who lived in New York City. He wrote to her and simply said that he enjoyed her comments. She wrote back. One year and one month of writing then took place and the two formed a loving relationship within these letters. But no matter how many times John asked, Hollis refused to send him a photograph. He was drafted overseas, but still the letters continued. Eventually he returned to the United States and they arranged to meet. The time was set – 3 p.m., and the place – Grand Central Station. She would wear a rose and he would wear his best dress uniform.

He arrived at the station as the clock struck 3 p.m. People began to leave the train that had just pulled in. And as he gazed, a lady started walking towards him; her figure was long and slim. Her blonde hair lay back in curls from her delicate ears; her eyes were as blue as flowers. Her lips and chin had a gentle firmness, and in her pale green suit she looked like springtime come alive.

John moved towards her but entirely forgetting to notice that she was not wearing a rose. As he got closer, a small provocative smile curved her lips and she whispered, "Going my way, sailor?"

Almost uncontrollably John made one step closer to her, and then he saw Hollis Maynell. She was standing almost directly behind the girl. She was a woman well past 50, she had greying hair tucked under a hat. She was more than plump and her thick-ankled feet were thrust into low-heeled shoes.

The girl in the pale green suit was quickly walking away. John was torn. What should he do? So keen was his desire to follow her and yet so deep was his longing for the woman whose spirit had truly companioned and upheld his own. And there she stood. Her pale, plump face was gentle and sensible; her grey eyes had a warm and kindly twinkle. But John didn't hesitate. He squared his shoulders and saluted, "I am Lt John Blanchard. I am so glad you could meet me. May I take you to dinner?"

The woman's face broadened into a tolerant smile. She said, "I don't know what this is about, son. But that young lady in the green suit who just went by, she begged me to wear this rose on my coat. And she said if you ask me to dinner, I should tell you she is waiting in the big restaurant across the street. She said it was some kind of test."

Did you enjoy the journey? Did you learn anything that you can add to your great pool of knowledge? I suspect not. But how do you *feel*? Stories move us, they operate on a level far deeper than simple cognition. And this is important because the latest research tells us that children are now exhibiting a nonlinear style of thinking. A mosaic. A generation that is wired for stories. This "Mosaic" or nonlinear style of thinking is demonstrated in the table opposite. The style of linear, sequential logic that has been categorized as left-brain activity is losing significance and the right-brain activities of intuition and narrative have reasserted themselves clamouring for prominence and insisting on involvement in life and learning for the first time in half a millennium. Stories communicate on a whole new level.

The differences between storytelling and linear teaching

STORYTELLING	LINEAR TEACHING
Inductive	Deductive
Accumulative	Assertive
Achieves authority	Assumes authority
Asks questions	Asserts answers
Assembles facts	Asserts concepts as facts
Builds on facts to find causes	Binds facts into categories
Constructive	Constrictive
Creative	Cognitive
Defers Assertions	Declares answers
Diagnoses reasons	Defends reason
Discovers causes	Declares conclusion
Expanding	Contracting
Explores, exposes	Explains, exhorts
Flexible, elastic	Firm, set
Intuitive	Intellectual
Invites participation	Imposes principles
Involves listeners in questions	Imparts answers
Open	Closed
Prophetic	Priestly
Practical	Perspective
Progressive	Protective
Reasonable	Reasoning
Relates	Restricts
Relational accent	Rational accent
Seeks causes, concepts, conclusions	States effects, conclusions
Seeks reasons, evidence, principles	States results, proofs

The Journey Has a Guide

When a story is told, rather than read, there is a whole different connection between storyteller and listener. Many objective studies have tested listener reactions to someone reading from a manuscript versus speaking extemporaneously and have concluded that with the latter there is 36 per cent more retention and that listeners are instantly more sympathetic and more attentive.[2] Bruno Bettelheim who undertook extensive study on the telling of fairy tales commented, "A story should be told rather than read. Extemporaneous speech makes the speaker seem more vulnerable and accessible and therefore more credible."[3]

Crib notes are fine, when you are telling a story but you're only allowed a maximum of ten key statements or prompts that can be placed on an A3 sheet and taped to the floor in front of you. No more or you'll be tempted to read. Below are the ten keywords or phrases to tell the story of "The Selfish Giant".

1. Every day after school
2. Giant returns
3. Nowhere to play
4. Spring does not come
5. Little boy under tree
6. Giant plays too
7. Asks after boy
8. Older
9. Winter again
10. Little boy returns.

Bettelheim also introduces another important aspect: the credibility of the storyteller. *Esse quam videri* is the Latin for *to be, rather than*

---

2 Lewis and Lewis in their 1983 book, *Inductive Communication*
3 *The Uses of Enchantment: The meaning and importance of Fairy Tales* (1977)

to appear. It is the personal credibility of the storyteller that validates the story.

When we communicate:

15 per cent of our message is to do with content

25 per cent of our message is to do with tone

60 per cent of our message is to do with who we are.[4]

When I stand in front of a group of children and speak, my message amounts to only 15 per cent of my overall communication. If my tone is not consistent with my message I will not communicate anything. If I am telling my story to a large crowd, but wish I was at home in my cosy house watching television, then who I am overrides my tone and message and again I communicate nothing. To put this another way, we could draw on the Zulu proverb:

"I can't hear what you are saying because who you are is shouting in my face."

Now, I know the stories in this book are hardly the manifesto of a major political party approaching an election, but the same principles apply. A storyteller whose heart is not in it will mess up the delivery of the story even if she delivers every word perfectly with dazzling enunciation, razor-sharp wit, and a range of regional accents! Who we are communicates. Be a credible storyteller by ensuring that you carry yourself with integrity. Be trustworthy. I may have told only 600 primary school children the story of Gladys Aylward travelling to China this morning, but they were assessing my personal credibility as I spoke and by the end they had decided if they could trust me. This is about far more than cognition. Therefore the storyteller needs to have a heart free of baggage and a sweet spirit – not at all easy to maintain.

---

4   Cited from *One Generation from Extinction*

The Journey Has to Start Somewhere

An effective first line is the hook. Get it wrong and there is no catch, the fish swims away.

> "High above the city on a tall column stood the statue of the happy prince."

So starts Oscar Wilde's "The Happy Prince", and we instantly find ourselves in a different world. Looking down a huge city stretching in all directions. But you can help it further. When delivering the line I stand still and regimental like a statue, with only the slightest hint of a wobble to illustrate that I am up very high.

Consider too the opening of the story of George and Mr Spencer.

> "It came as quite a surprise when George walked into the room and proclaimed, "Mum, Dad…""

And the opening line to Tolstoy's "The Shoemaker".

> "The shoemaker wasn't very rich…"

They draw the listener into a new world. A new reality. The journey can now continue. The listener is ready to journey with you. They have been hooked.

The Journey Itself

Take a look around. Describe what you see. That knight riding beside you isn't just quiet, he is mocking you with stony silence. You occupy two roles. You are the artist, you are painting the scene. But you are also the servant of the story. When the story tells us that "Telemachus shouted at the top of his voice, 'this is not right'" – then the story expects a shout. And when "with his dying breath Telemachus whispers, 'this is not right'" – then that is what is expected. Use your voice. Whisper, project, pause, and then use your greatest tool, be silent. Silence is our friend. Particularly with a large crowd. Any head teacher will tell you that to control a whole school assembly you do not raise your voice, you drop it.

This book gives you the text of each of the stories, but they are alive: they can take different forms and shapes depending on who is telling them. Here are a few more keys:

- Use precisely the right word. Say it was oval, not it was sort of round.

- Use specific, not generic words. Say pinto pony – not just horse. Say shack, mansion, lean-to, not just building.

- Use descriptive words. Say the wind whined and clawed at the corner of the house, not the wind blew hard.

- Use action verbs. Say he tore out, breezed out, strolled out – not went out.

- Use short, forceful Anglo-Saxon words. Say he died – not he passed away – not contiguous.

- Use words found in your listeners' vocabulary. Say swollen, not distended; I like you, not I hold you in high esteem.

- Use onomatopoeic words that imitate natural sounds. Say buzz, soothe, lull, smooth, bang.

- Use words with significant contemporary meaning, say home, not residence; meal not repast.

- Avoid clichés, religious jargon, trade talk, and stale fancy phrases. Only the story "Runaway" starts with "It was a dark and stormy night". And that out of a sense of sheer mischief.

A few more storytelling aids

Repetition

Traditional stories such as "The Three Little Pigs" rely on repetition and formula: "I'll huff and I'll puff" repeated again and again. Similar systems are used when Walter asks, "Not chicken are you?" in the story of "Bushy and Rusty". They are there to aid in memorization. But they also build tension. A similar technique can be seen in the "drip, drip, drip" of "The Happy Prince". And this leads to our next aid…

The power of three

Three drips. Two doesn't work, and neither does four. Try this out if you don't believe me. Typically there are three sons in the adventure stories, there are three encounters with Farmer Brown in "Bushy and Rusty", there are three "needs" in "The Happy Prince," three stages to "The Young King." There is undoubtedly a clever reason why, but sometimes it is enough to recognize that it works and go with it.

Connect with the main characters

You need to understand the main characters. Become friends with them. Know how they will respond in given situations. Understand why. They may have been written as two-dimensional characters, but you can give them life. Let them exist in the imagination of your hearers. Allow your characters to live.

Use the available space

If you are presenting to a large crowd, use the stage/platform/front of the area as a timeline. This is particularly useful if you are telling a story out of chronological order. Certain things happen at certain points on the stage. This will work as a memory aid to you. You'll remember certain things in certain places. But it will also help the audience. They will come to associate various parts of the physical space with various aspects/stages of the journey and it will become a memory aid to the audience too. Remember, you are performing a story. Think performance. Also think through things that detract. The wrong gestures and mannerisms can get in the way of the story.

What the Journey Reveals

There have been long drawn out theological debates that have run for centuries around whether there are degrees of sin. I am not sure. But I can tell you the worst sin of them all is to say the words:

"THIS MEANS, BOYS AND GIRLS…"

If you ever say these words at the end of one of these stories I hope they give you detention. It is the storyteller's greatest crime. **LISTEN! GREAT STORIES DON'T NEED TO BE EXPLAINED**. Oscar Wilde's "The Selfish Giant" is an incredible piece of storytelling. When I first told the story I was tempted at the end to ask the school, "Who was that little boy?" The result was a few answers and the end of the assembly. A few years later when I repeated the story, I ended with, "I can't tell you who the little boy is but maybe you'll work it out." This time there were lots more conversations and a general buzz of discovery after the assembly. But now I stop at the end of the assembly, I ask everyone to think about the story, I say a short prayer for the school, and I sit down. No explanation. No leading the children in a certain direction. No clues! The results have been staggering. Children who had no friends because they were unkind understood from the story that kindness means friends, and it worked. Children worked out who the little boy was and why he was hurt. But one head teacher broke my heart when she phoned to say that the little boy who was struggling with the death of his granddad now knew that Jesus would look after him! That's the power of the story. To communicate to dozens of people in different ways at he same time. Stories are truly powerful. And if you have never read "The Selfish Giant" you'll have no idea what any of this paragraph means, but the stories are coming soon!

Bettelheim writes:

> The story communicates to the child an intuitive, subconscious understanding of his own nature and of what his future may hold if he develops his positive potentials… one must never *explain* to the child the meanings of fairy tales.[5]

Tolkien, the master storyteller and creator of Middle Earth, goes further and makes an interesting observation in our world of PowerPoint and video projectors.

> Illustrations do little good to fairy stories… If a story says, *he climbed a hill and saw a river in the valley below,* the illustrator may catch, or nearly catch, his own vision of such a scene, but every hearer of the words will have his own picture, and it will be made out of all the hills and rivers and dales he has ever seen.[6]

Great stories are those that address us, draw us in as part of larger stories beyond our own selves, act as a corrective to the distorted

---

5   *The Uses of Enchantment: The meaning and importance of Fairy Tales* (1977)
6   From his 1965 book, *Tree and Leaf*

stories that seek to claim us, and give new meaning to our own stories.[7]

The same principle holds true concerning the alluring pieces of storytelling within the gospels of Matthew, Mark, Luke, and John that together form the "Jesus Story". Jesus is rarely listed in the books of great preachers, yet the gospels record instances of people of varying ages travelling large distances to hear him speak. However, he does not use the deductive styles that define preachers from the eighteenth century onward. He rarely preached without a story, and most of those were *parables*. The New Testament records thirty-three to seventy-seven parables of Jesus.[8] He does not use them merely as teasers, light introductions to get his hearers listening for what he really wants to say; they are often the primary expression of his message. The story of the Good Samaritan forms a sermon on compassion, the Prodigal Son teaches forgiveness. When Jesus preaches, the *narrative* doesn't back up his message, it *is* his message.

Reflections on the Journey

The interesting, frustrating, glorious thing about life is that it's messy. A piece of oratory that simply presents cold, clinical facts in a logical sequential way cannot capture life. But a story is not like that. There are no clean edges, few situations where everything is resolved, and very few neat endings. We simply take our reader to an inn, a place where they may well take the story further, or pause to reflect on the journey so far; it's a stopover point, a place from which they will begin their next journey.

One of my personal favourite storytellers is Susan Howatch. In the final novel of her popular Starbridge series she uses one of her

---

7   The root thought came from John Hull, Emeritus Professor of Education University of Birmingham

8   Depending on which definition of parable is used.

characters to talk about the creative process. It really does sound like the storyteller in action:

> But no matter how much the mess and distortion make you want to despair, you can't abandon the work because you're chained to it, it's absolutely woven into your soul and you know you can never rest until you've brought truth out of all the distortion, and beauty out of the mess – but it's agony, agony, agony – while simultaneously being the most wonderful and rewarding experience in the world – and that's the creative process which so few people understand.
>
> It makes an indestructible sort of fidelity, an insane sort of hope, an indescribable sort of... well, it's love, isn't it? There's no other word for it. That's the way it is. That's creation, you can't create without waste and mess and sheer undiluted slog. You can't create without pain. It's all part of the process. It's the nature of things. So in the end every major disaster, every tiny error, every wrong turning, every fragment of discarded clay, all the blood, the sweat and tears – everything has a meaning. I give it meaning. I reuse, reshape, recast all that goes wrong so that in the end nothing is wasted and nothing is without significance and nothing ceases to be precious.[9]

Am I overstating all this? After all, it is just storytelling. Try it and see. On a few occasions I have had the privilege of telling stories in front of more than 5,000 people in an auditorium and I can assure you that there is nothing quite like that moment when thousands of people from all ages and all walks of life are sitting in silence, with mouths open, hanging on your every word, desperate to know where

---

9   Susan Howatch, *Absolute Truths*, London, HarperCollins, 1994.

the story will lead them. Enjoy it and see the power of the story to transform.

Stories will take you to the depths of sorrow – I have watched as the stories of Gelert and of the Signalman's Son take a whole school to hysterical laughter and then to actual tears and then for one of the stories at least, back to laughter. You'll need to read them to see which does what!

And of course there is one more dimension. Now that you have understood all this, maybe you can tell your own stories, new stories, stories to captivate and enthral, new stories to make us laugh and cry, new characters to enjoy.

Are You Sitting Comfortably...?

Curiously, this is not just an expression. Some children would love to listen to your story but can't! Allow me to explain by way of an example. Several years ago I visited a project run out of a community centre in one of the lower socio-economic parts of Sydney. For the first few months of running the project the leaders could not get the children to listen. They were truly wild. These children didn't just write on the toilet doors, they set fire to them. The change came one evening when a leader began to chat to the children and realized that many of them hadn't eaten a proper meal for several days and would probably go several more days before they got fed again. The children couldn't sit still because they were hungry.

Psychologist Abraham Maslow first introduced his concept of a hierarchy of needs in 1943, in a paper called "A Theory of Human Motivation". This hierarchy, commonly displayed as a pyramid (see page 28), suggests that we all have basic needs and that these have to be met in an order of importance. The lowest level of the pyramid focuses on the most basic physical needs – for food, clothing, housing – just as highlighted in the Sydney project.

Once these lower-level needs have been met, people can move on to the next level of needs, which are for safety and protection. So it's also worth asking the question, are my listeners sitting comfortably? What needs to be done to make them feel comfortable? Here I have only touched on a little of Maslow's theory which continues to influence those interested in psychology even today.

A graphic interpretation of Maslow's Hierarchy of Needs from the most basic to the less essential.

That project in Sydney now feeds dozens of hungry children copious amounts of pasta at the start of every session. The result is well fed children who are keen to listen. So take the time to discover what the extra need is. Maybe you simply need to spend time with your listeners, time making them feel secure. It's worth exploring, don't take anything for granted in our twenty-first century world.

Stories in
Different Contexts

Stories can play an important part in a wide variety of contexts. Below, we consider stories in the context of schools, as part of an all-age church service, and used with the individual at bedtime.

Schools

When my daughter started school it was an emotional morning in the Griffiths household. She was excited. My wife and I were nervous. She put on her little school uniform. She collected her packed lunch, with the obligatory logo. She put on her new shoes and took her mother's hand for the short journey to school. She loved it. She talked about it all evening. Then, just after her bedtime story, she looked very serious and said, "Daddy, do I have to go to school for long?"

The answer was clearly yes. Yes for her and for the hundreds of thousands of other children who make their way to school every day. Yes. For at least the next fourteen years. It is the place she will spend a considerable part of her early life, and the place she will hear the most stories.

The Teacher in School

And the people who tell most of those stories in schools are teachers. The majority of teacher training courses focus on teaching teachers how to teach their class. Obvious? Well yes, but that means they are not taught how to stand in front of the whole school – and worse still, in front of other teachers – to take school assemblies. This book is designed to take away the panic. It provides the stories that are in easy reach. I have spent enough time in school staff rooms to know that there is never enough time. And when time is of the essence, it is preparation for assembly that is put to the bottom of the list. This book means you can still deliver a great assembly with very little preparation. Obviously, the more preparation time the better the story will be (well, most of the time).

The Church in School

The UK still allows us access to schools to take assemblies. In fact, the Education Act requires that there is an act of collective worship that is predominantly Christian in nature every day. Most schools in Australia and New Zealand are also open to outside input. What a privilege. There is an opportunity to allow children to get a glimpse of God; to allow boys and girls to encounter Jesus. If every vicar, pastor, and minister took the time to visit their local school just once a month then every child in the country would receive regular Christian input. And it doesn't have to be more than once a month. Most ministers are frantically busy. But a monthly input can make a significant difference. Nine visits a year is all it takes. It would give the church huge favour with the school, and open the door to so many more opportunities. But more importantly, it will allow boys and girls the opportunity to encounter God.

How about some facts:

- 39 per cent of our churches have nobody in them under the age of eleven;
- 49 per cent of our churches have nobody in them aged twelve to fourteen;
- 59 per cent of our churches have nobody in them aged fourteen to nineteen.[10]

And one more:

- There are 54,000 children in Church of England schools in the Oxford diocese alone. That's more than the number of people in the Oxford Diocese's churches on a typical Sunday morning.[11]

If the church is to communicate Jesus to children, then it will need to go where they are. And, of course, this is not just about church schools. In fact, part of the vision for schools ministry must be to raise the standard for all. That's what's great about the Oxford Diocesan Mission statement: "The transformation of all human life under God." It categorically states that God will not be restricted to a church or even a church hall. Jesus wants to permeate everything. And since his heart has always been to allow children to come to him, he wants to permeate our schools.

And if churches give good input – input that is not "over the top" and is interesting and communicates well – then they will find the door wide open. But don't underestimate the need to provide good assemblies. Often churches have assumed that they have not

10   Statistics by Peter Brierley, cited from my book, *One Generation from Extinction*.
11   Oxford Diocesan Board of Education statistics, 2005.

been invited back because the school is trying to keep Christianity out. Actually, it's more likely that the school is trying to keep boring assemblies out! It's hard work keeping hundreds of children well behaved and quiet when the person at the front is dull. Assemblies that radiate life and love and joy and wonder will always be appreciated.

There's a need to be interesting. And being interesting opens doors. In the United States, where access to schools is not always so free, the engaging storyteller will still find an opening. Just be very careful to avoid, "this means, boys and girls…"

What about Sunday church (all-age worship)?

I am regularly told on my travels to other churches that it is the worst-attended service of the month. They are talking about their family service, the time (whether monthly, termly, or just for special occasions) when all ages gather together. How can that be? It's supposed to be a vibrant, uplifting, joyful experience – no, really! And in some places it is. For some churches, the family service is the most popular and best attended. In many communities, the family service has proved to be *the way* the church has reconnected with its communities. Some churches have gone from close to extinction to thriving communities, primarily because of their ability to develop a good, engaging, life-giving family service.

It's not possible to communicate to a four-year-old and a forty-four-year-old in the same place at the same time. This has been the argument of the educationalists for over a century now. But Jesus did it. And Jesus did it all the time. Jesus was able to stand in the middle of a large crowd and speak, and the oldest person would understand at their level, and the middle-aged at theirs, and the child would be so captivated by the message he would bring his lunch of bread and fish to Jesus and ask, "Can you do anything with this?"

How? Jesus told stories. It is *the way* to communicate across the generations. It is not confined to nationality, socio-economic groups, and certainly not to age. The power of the story to creep past the intellect and touch the heart is obvious to anyone who has observed a storyteller in action.

And at bedtime

The bond established between storyteller and listener is an important part of storytelling. And stories that you tell to your children, where the protagonist's name is replaced by your child's name, are the most exciting of all. The lived experience. These stories will form a connection for years to come, and one day your child may sit beside their own child's bed and utter the words: "Your grandfather used to tell me this story…" A generational bond is established through the art of storytelling.

The true strength of narrative comes when it is allowed to be woven into the experiences and current realities of the child, allowing the child to learn the lessons of the story for themselves, allowing the morals of the story to slowly merge with their own reality and become relevant specifically to them.

This is a book of stories. Enjoy sharing them.

Antonio the Juggler

Let me take you back hundreds of years to Italy, and a delightful town called Sorrento. In those days, Sorrento only had two places worth visiting – the church and the market. The market was always very busy. So many things to buy; pasta and cheese and fine clothes, and so many different types of wine! Lots of people selling and lots of people buying. The stallholders would sell anything, and the people would buy anything. The church could only be described as beautiful. It had enormous stained-glass windows stretching up to a very high and magnificently decorated ceiling. When the sun shone, wonderful colours glimmered around the great hall, bathing everything in the most astonishing colours. At the front there stood a statue of Mary, and in front of Mary, a statue of Jesus. The statue showed Jesus at about seven years old. And it was said that this statue looked very sad indeed.

In the town there lived a young boy. His name was Antonio. Antonio was six years old. He was an orphan; he had no mother or father, and would sleep every night in doorways in the marketplace. He was dressed in rags and had no money – but he was happy. And he could do something very special. Antonio could juggle. He would juggle apples and oranges and potatoes, he would juggle tomatoes, pears and even cucumbers. He could juggle anything. Every day, he would stand in the marketplace and juggle, and the people of Sorrento would put money in his bowl; money he used to buy food.

One day a troupe of travelling performers came to Sorrento and began to set up in the market square. Very soon the performance began. Everyone clapped and cheered as first the acrobats did cartwheels and handstands, then a lady sang the loveliest song that Antonio had ever heard. After that, a man stepped forward to do some magic tricks, and finally another man stretched a rope across the market square and walked across the rope, balancing above everyone's heads. It was the most extraordinary sight.

Antonio thought, "It must be great to be a performer. This is the life for me." And so he approached the leader and asked if he could join the travelling performers. The leader frowned.

"We don't need a beggar. Go away!" came the stern reply.

But Antonio was persistent. "But I can do something special," he said. "I can juggle."And Antonio began to juggle.

The leader smiled. "Not bad. With a bit of practise, you may turn out to be quite good. You may join us. Don't expect to be paid, but we will give you one meal a day, and the company of the finest performers in Italy."

That was one meal more than Antonio was getting, so he joined the performers and began to travel Italy. He practised long and hard until he became very good indeed. Then one day the lead performer gave him a clown outfit and told him that it was time for Antonio to juggle for the crowds. After the lady who sang the lovely song had finished, the leader stood in front of the people and announced:

"Ladies and gentlemen, boys and girls, for your joy and entertainment I give you the greatest juggler in the whole world. Antonio!"

Antonio, now dressed as a clown, walked onto the platform. He juggled with sticks, with plates, with rings, then with burning torches.

Finally he threw a red ball into the air, then an orange one, then a yellow, then a green, then blue, then purple. With the balls rotating so quickly they looked like a rainbow, he proclaimed, "Now, ladies and gentlemen, it's time for the sun in the heavens." And up it went, the big golden ball. Nobody knew how he did it, but it looked like the most amazing rainbow spinning around with a golden ball hovering above.

The people cheered and cheered. "He is the best juggler in all of Italy!" they said.

After several years, Antonio left the performers and began to travel by himself. He would enter a town and very quickly the people would gather around. It was always the same routine. He juggled with sticks, then plates, then rings, then burning torches, and finally up would go the red ball into the air, then an orange one, then a yellow, then a green, then blue, then purple. "Now, ladies and gentlemen," he would proclaim, "it's time for the sun in the heavens." And up it went, the big golden ball. All the people cheered and cheered, and they gave Antonio more money than he had ever seen.

He performed in front of dukes and princes, kings and queens and always the same thing: sticks, plates, rings, burning torches, the coloured balls, and the sun in the heavens.

Antonio became very rich and very famous. He no longer wore rags. Now he dressed in the best robes, and no longer slept in doorways, but in the finest guest houses. He no longer ate scraps, but only the most delicious food.

One day he was eating his lunch in a field between two villages. Two priests walked by.

"Sirs, why don't you join me for some lunch?" Antonio called. "I have plenty."

The priests were hungry and appreciated the offer. As they ate, Antonio enquired, "Where are you going?"

"We're going throughout Italy spreading the love of God. Maybe you could come with us?"

Antonio shook his head. "That's good for you, but I'm just a juggler. I go from town to town making people smile."

"Maybe it's the same thing," one of the priests said. "Maybe when you bring joy to people you bring joy to God."

"That may be so," Antonio smiled, "but I must be on my way." With that, he collected his things and off he set.

Antonio spent many, many years travelling and juggling. But there came a time when things were hard in Italy. The harvest failed, food became scarce, and people were struggling to feed their families. And very soon nobody had time for the juggler, no matter how good he was.

"We've seen your tricks before, old man!" – for Antonio by this time had grown very old – "Go away." He went from town to town, but nobody wanted to see his juggling. And then, one day it happened – in front of a disinterested crowd, he dropped the golden ball. The crowds laughed, but not with joy. They drove him out of the town, calling him names.

"The clown who can't juggle!" they all laughed.

Antonio walked away. He came to a stream; the old man sat down, removed his clown face and put his juggling things in a bag. It was over. He wandered around, not knowing where to go. All his money had gone, and his clothes became rags again. When the cold weather came, Antonio decided it was time to go home, and set out for Sorrento. He walked for many days, eventually arriving in Sorrento in the middle of the night. Everywhere was locked up. Everywhere except the church. He went in and, finding a corner at the back, he went to sleep.

He was woken the next morning to the sound of music. As he looked around, he saw the old church was full of people. They were singing and, in turn, they were bringing gifts and placing them in front of the statue of Mary and Jesus.

"What is going on?" Antonio asked someone.

"Old man, don't you know anything? It's harvest festival. They're bringing their gifts to God."

Antonio stood and watched.

At the end, everyone went home. Antonio walked to the front and looked at the statue of Jesus. "You look so sad," he said to the statue. "All these wonderful gifts and still you look so sad. I wish I had a gift I could bring you."

And then it occurred to Antonio that maybe he did have a gift. He thought, "I used to make people happy." He emptied his bag onto the floor, knelt before the statue, put on his clown face and began to juggle. He juggled with sticks, then plates, then rings, then burning torches. He had never juggled this well in his life. His heart was beating fast. "This is for you, little child!" And he threw a red ball into the air, then an orange one, then a yellow, then a green, then blue, then purple. "And now," he proclaimed, "it's time for the sun in the heavens." And up went the big golden ball.

When he had finished, he lay down in front of the statue.

Antonio lay there until later that day, when two priests came in. They rushed up to Antonio. One of them knelt beside him. Turning to the other priest, he said, "He's dead. His heart has stopped."

But the other priest wasn't listening. He had his mouth open and was stumbling backwards. He was pointing at the statue. For there on the face of Jesus was a great big smile. And in his hands he held a large golden ball!

It's a strange idea that by making others happy we can make God happy. It's a strange idea that by giving our gifts to others to make them happy we can make God happy. It's a strange idea, but I think it's true.

And if you visit the Italian town of Sorrento today, and you go to that little church, you'll see a statue of Mary and of Jesus. Jesus looks as if he's about seven years of age. And if you look closely at the statue of Jesus, you'll see he's smiling. And in his hands he holds a golden ball.

A Dog Called Gelert

It is said that just over 800 years ago in Wales, there lived a prince whose name was Llewelyn. Llewelyn had two things that he prized above everything else. The first was his huge hunting dog. He had named him Gelert. He slept in the great hall of the castle in front of the large fire. Everyone in the prince's castle was frightened of him.

The prince had good cause to love Gelert. On more than one occasion, wolves that lived in the woods around the castle had tried to kill Llewelyn, but Gelert was always too fast for them, and would never let them near his master. On the one occasion that a wolf had had the boldness to run out into the clearing and leap at the prince, Gelert had leapt and killed the wolf in mid-air.

Llewelyn loved his dog dearly, but the most important person in his life was his son. He loved his son more than he loved anyone else in his entire nation. His son was nine months old and was the cutest of babies, but very naughty; he would throw his food off his plate, he was sick over his nursemaid, he tried to throw his shoes out of the window. But he had a really sweet smile, which meant however much trouble he got into, he could just smile and giggle, and no one would tell him off.

A Dog Called Gelert

Gelert was the fiercest dog in Wales. Nobody would dare go near him. One growl and they would run. Everyone was afraid – well, nearly everyone; nobody had told the baby to be afraid of Gelert, so he wasn't. One day the little baby crawled out of the nursery and into the great hall. He then crawled over to the dog. Gelert gave a low growl, but the baby giggled and moved closer. Gelert growled more loudly. The baby giggled again and moved closer. Gelert was getting more and more annoyed, but the baby kept getting closer and closer, giggling the entire time.

Then the baby looked up into Gelert's face. The dog looked down at him and gave a mighty bark, but instead of crying – as you might expect – the baby grabbed the dog's ears, and when Gelert stood back up the baby was hanging by Gelert's ears. Gelert didn't know what to do. Everyone was scared of him and that's the way he liked it. How come this baby wasn't? Gelert just stood there with the baby hanging from his ears and began to cry until the baby let go and crawled away.

The next day the baby crawled over and grabbed Gelert's tail. He started swinging backwards and forwards on it. When he got a bit older, the baby started crawling onto Gelert's back and riding around on him. On another occasion, the baby went missing altogether and nobody could work out where he had gone. They searched high and low in every room, and still they couldn't find the baby. Eventually, somebody spotted him. He had crawled next to Gelert and was fast asleep, curled up with the dog.

The nursemaid went to pick the baby up, but Gelert opened his mouth and let out a mighty bark which sent the nursemaid running as fast as she could. So that's where the baby stayed until he had slept long enough, and then he crawled away from the dog so the nursemaid could change his nappy.

Gelert and the baby became so attached that whenever the prince would go off on a hunting trip, he would leave Gelert behind to look after the baby.

The woods that surrounded the castle were very thick, and from time to time wolves would wander out of them and make their way towards the castle to see if there was something to eat. One day, a very large and hungry wolf made his way to the castle, and as he approached he sniffed the air; he could smell something sweet. He jumped up at one of the castle windows and looked in. Gelert was asleep beneath the wall so the wolf couldn't see him, but what he could see excited him. There was a baby lying in a crib. The wolf licked his lips and opened his mouth, revealing his sharp teeth. He saw the nursemaid, but he was in no rush. He could wait until she left, and then he'd pounce.

A long time went by and the wolf waited patiently. It was late in the afternoon, and the wolf could hear the prince in the distance, returning from the hunt. The wolf knew that if he didn't attack soon it would be too late. But then the nursemaid went to get the baby some milk. It was the wolf's opportunity. He flexed his muscles and then sprang at the crib. He thought he would grab the baby in his massive jaws, and turn and escape back into the woods.

He flew through the air, his mouth open. He was just about to grab the baby when Gelert awoke. Gelert instinctively dived towards the wolf. He was aiming for his throat, but only managed to knock the wolf in the ribs and send him hurtling against one of the walls. The wolf was furious and ran at Gelert with all his strength. They barked and growled. The wolf jumped on top of Gelert and it looked as if he would kill the great dog, but Gelert used all his strength and pinned the wolf to the ground. Then they tumbled and turned. The furniture was knocked over, the crib was turned over so that the baby ended up underneath, the sofa was turned over, and there was blood splattered on the walls. Finally, the wolf made a last leap at Gelert and it looked as if he was going to win. But Gelert was too quick, and with the speed that only a hunting dog has, he dodged the wolf and sank his teeth into him. It was all over. The wolf was dead.

A Dog Called Gelert

The prince returned to his castle, and the first thing he wanted to do was see his son. But when he came to the nursery he could not believe his eyes. The room was a mess, there was blood everywhere and the baby was nowhere to be seen. The wolf was out of sight behind the overturned sofa, and there was Gelert crawling towards him with blood all over his body. The prince had the kind of temper which just exploded and the first thing he thought was, "Gelert's killed the baby!"

His anger exploded, he grabbed his gun, pointed it at Gelert and – BANG! He killed his best hunting dog.

The prince was devastated by what had happened. His son was dead and so was beloved Gelert. The two things he prized above anything else were gone.

The prince began to cry, but through his sobs he heard a faint cry coming from somewhere in the room. He searched frantically to find out where the sound had come from. He lifted up the crib and there, to his amazement, was his son. The prince picked up the baby and as he did, he saw the body of the dead wolf. Then the prince realized what had happened, and he was devastated.

Because he couldn't control his temper he had killed not only his best hunting dog, but the dog who had saved his son's life.

The Shoemaker

The shoemaker wasn't very rich. His house had one room and in that one room he ate, slept and, of course, made and mended shoes. But neither was he very poor, for in his room he had a warm bed, a comfortable chair, a hot fire for cooking, and all the tools he needed for making and mending shoes. With the money he received, he bought soup to eat and his favourite coffee to drink.

It was Christmas Eve, and the shoemaker was in his warm room looking out onto the market. Although he had plenty of food and some of his favourite coffee, inside he felt sad. Tomorrow would be Christmas Day and he would be all alone. His wife had died several years before, and his sons and daughters had all got married and moved a long way away.

"Dear, dear me," sighed the old shoemaker. "What will I do?"

He reached up to his bookshelf and took down a book.

"Maybe this will take my mind off it," he said as he sat in his chair and began to read. The book was his Bible and in it he turned to the story of Christmas. He read about how Mary and Joseph travelled all the way to Bethlehem and how Mary was going to give birth but there was nowhere to stay.

"Oh dear, dear," said the shoemaker, "if they had come to my village they could have stayed with me."

He read about the shepherds and wise men.

"Oh, what a wonderful story," he said. "All those wise men bringing those lovely gifts to Jesus. Oh dear, if I were to bring a gift to Jesus, I wonder what it would be? Oh dear, dear, what would I give?"

He thought about this for some time, and then he remembered. He reached up to his top shelf and took down a box. He took the lid off. Inside there were the tiniest shoes you have ever seen. They were wonderful; they had the most intricate stitches and were made out of the finest leather.

"Yes, I would give Jesus these," he whispered.

He returned to his comfortable chair and continued to read. Maybe it was the heat or maybe it was because he had been working so hard all day, but before long he was fast asleep. He hadn't slept long when he heard a voice: "Shoemaker, you wanted me to visit you and you wanted to give me a present. Tomorrow I will visit you. Be ready."

The shoemaker jumped up. "Who was that?"

Of course, he knew it was Jesus. The shoemaker was so excited. Jesus was coming to visit him. He nodded off again but didn't sleep too well. He was thinking of Christmas Day and getting ready for Jesus. He woke very early. It was still dark. When was Jesus coming? And how would he recognize him? Jesus hadn't always been a baby; he grew up, he died on a cross, he rose from the grave; some people said that he was the Son of God, the King of all kings. How would he know him? The shoemaker looked out of the window. Where was Jesus? He looked out of the window again. Still no sign of Jesus. He went to his fire.

"I'll make some coffee while I'm waiting," he said to himself. "Maybe Jesus would like some coffee when he comes."

He went to the window again and looked out. Who was this walking up the street? It was very hard to see; it was still dark, and there was a thick frosty mist. Was it Jesus? As he watched, the shoemaker saw the shape of a road sweeper coming towards him. The shoemaker was very disappointed, but carried on making his coffee.

Every so often he would make his way to the window and check up and down the street. Still no sign of Jesus, but that road sweeper looked very cold. He was right outside the shoemaker's shop and was clapping his hands together, trying to make them warm. The shoemaker was waiting for Jesus, but the road sweeper looked so cold he felt he should invite him in. He opened the door and called out, "Excuse me! Would you like to come in to get warm?"

The road sweeper seemed surprised. But he was freezing, and any offer of warmth was welcome. So he made his way into the shoemaker's house and began to warm himself by the fire.

"Would you like some coffee?" asked the kind shoemaker.

The road sweeper reached over and took his coffee.

"Merry Christmas," said the shoemaker.

"Thank you very much. This is all the Christmas I'll get," replied the road sweeper.

The shoemaker kept looking out of the window.

"Are you waiting for someone?" enquired the road sweeper.

The shoemaker told him all about the voice.

"Well, I hope he comes!" The road sweeper made his way to the door, smiled for the first time, and then left the shop.

Morning had arrived now, and although it was still very cold some people were beginning to venture onto the streets. The shoemaker kept looking for Jesus, but still there was no sign. Then he noticed something unusual. There, walking towards him up the street, was a young lady pushing a pram. She looked frozen. She had obviously walked a long way. The shoemaker leaned out of the door.

"Excuse me! You look very cold. Would you like to come in to get warm?"

The girl seemed afraid.

"Don't worry," said the shoemaker. "I have many children and grandchildren. Come on in."

The girl was wary, but she was also freezing. So she made her way into the shoemaker's home. He helped her to lift in the pram. The shoemaker looked down at the baby who looked very cold. And then the shoemaker noticed the baby had nothing on his feet; his feet were nearly blue with cold.

"Where are his shoes?" exclaimed the shoemaker.

The girl was embarrassed but explained, "I don't have enough money to buy shoes. We used to live in the next village, but because I have no money I have been thrown out of my house. Now I must walk to my sister's home, ten miles away."

The shoemaker knew what he should do. "But I am keeping that present for Jesus!" he said to himself. Then he looked at the baby's little cold feet. And he gave in. He decided that there was nothing else for it. He stretched up to the top shelf and took down the box. He opened it and placed the tiny shoes on the baby's feet. They were wonderful; they had the most intricate stitches – and they fitted perfectly. The mother was so thankful. She couldn't stop saying thank you. But all the time the shoemaker kept checking the window.

"Are you waiting for someone?" asked the girl.

The shoemaker told her of the voice the night before.

"I hope Jesus comes," she said. She smiled at the shoemaker and then made her way out of the shop.

It was beginning to get busy in the street now, with people visiting relatives. Last-minute Christmas presents were being dropped off. People were going to join their families for dinner. But there was still no sign of Jesus. The shoemaker saw many beggars, and to them he gave some money and he saw many poor people and to them he gave something to eat, and he saw people who were lonely, so he invited them in to chat, but there was no sign of Jesus.

Then the evening came and the thick frosty mist returned to the village. The shoemaker locked his door. It was too late for Jesus now. He felt very sad. Maybe he had dreamt the entire thing. He went to his comfortable chair and tried to go to sleep. But he felt so very miserable.

"Dear, dear me. I wish Jesus had come," he muttered.

He closed his eyes and tried to go to sleep. Then the voice came back again, the same voice as the night before: "Shoemaker, kind shoemaker. I came to you many times. I came disguised as the road sweeper and you gave me something to drink and a fire to warm my hands. I came as the beggars and the poor and you gave me food and money. And I came as the baby, and you gave me some shoes. Thank you, kind shoemaker. Because you have helped these people, you have helped me."

The shoemaker was so happy. "Jesus did come."

It was the best Christmas he had ever had.

The Happy Prince

High above the city on a tall column stood the statue of the Happy Prince. Now, the prince wasn't an ordinary statue. His eyes were made of bright blue stones called sapphires and at his side he wore a sword with a brilliant red stone at its hilt, called a ruby. From the bottom of his feet to the top of his head he was covered in the finest gold. And there he stood, looking over the city.

Far away, a small swallow decided it was time for him to fly south for the winter. He knew that he had waited too long and if he didn't leave soon, winter would come and he would die. So the swallow spread his wings and began his long journey. After several hours of flying, it began to get dark and the swallow knew he would have to find somewhere to spend the night. By this time he was high above the city and there below he could see the statue of the Happy Prince.

"That'll make a fine bedroom," he thought. "It will be nice to sleep in a bedroom with golden walls high above a city."

The swallow flew down, positioned himself at the feet of the prince, pulled his wing over his head, and began to drop off to sleep. A few minutes later he felt DRIP, DRIP, DRIP on his head.

"Oh no," he thought. "It's raining; winter has come already." The swallow looked up, but the sky was clear; there wasn't a cloud to be seen, just a bright autumn moon.

He lowered his head, pulled his wing over and tried to go to sleep again. A few minutes later, he felt DRIP, DRIP, DRIP on his head. "What is going on?" He looked up, but again the sky was clear. Then he looked up into the face of the prince. There, running down his face, were great big wet tears.

"Who are you?" asked the swallow, being a very inquisitive little bird.

"I'm the Happy Prince," the prince replied.

"Well, you don't look very happy. Why are you crying?"

"You see," the prince began, "when I was alive and had a heart of flesh instead of this heart of lead, I lived in the finest castle. The walls were of the finest gold. The floor was covered with the loveliest rugs and it was always warm. I wore the finest clothes and always had the very best food to eat. And I thought everyone else was exactly the same. I thought everyone had fine homes, lovely clothes, and plenty of food. But now that I can see the entire city I know that isn't true. Only today I looked out over the city and saw a little boy who is very ill. He was asking his mother for something to make him better, but she didn't have any money to buy medicine. He asked for something to drink, but all she had was water from the river. And it was probably the river water that made him sick in the first place. So tonight the little boy is crying, and his mother doesn't know what to do."

"That's really sad," said the swallow. "Is there something I can do to help?"

"Would you help, kind swallow? Would you?"

"Of course," the swallow replied, "but tomorrow I must fly south or the winter will come and I will die. But for now, what can I do?"

The prince instructed the swallow to fly up onto his sword and remove the ruby from its hilt. "Take it and fly with it to the boy's mother. With it she will be able to buy lots of medicine."

The swallow did as he was asked. The next day he flew to the house and dropped the ruby. The mother picked it up and was very excited. She had never seen a ruby before, but she knew that she could now buy all the medicine she needed. She didn't know that it had come from the swallow, she didn't know it had come from the Happy Prince. The swallow flew back to the prince and reported all that had happened. The prince smiled. It was now beginning to get quite cold, but the swallow felt very warm inside.

As night was already approaching, the swallow commented, "Prince, it is too late for me to fly south now, so I will spend one more night with you, but tomorrow I must fly south for the winter."

The swallow pulled his wing over his head and began to drop off to sleep. This would be his last night with the prince, or so he thought, until he felt DRIP, DRIP, DRIP on his head.

"Now what?" he thought. He looked up and there, running from the face of the Happy Prince, were great big wet tears.

"Prince, now what's wrong?" asked the exasperated swallow. The prince began to tell his new story: "Today I looked over the city and there in a little attic room was a young man. He was trying to finish a play for the theatre. But he won't be able to finish it now; it's too cold and he can't afford firewood until he finishes the play. And he has no more paper. And no money to buy either. So there he sits, shivering in his attic room."

The swallow really did need to fly south soon, but he was a very kind-hearted bird and so again he offered to help. "What can I do, dear Prince?"

The prince said, "Swallow, please fly onto my shoulder and take out one of my sapphire eyes and fly with it to the young man."

The swallow was horrified. He protested, but eventually gave in, and taking the sapphire he flew with it to the young man. He dropped the sapphire through a gap in the window and flew off. The young man had no idea where the precious stone had come from; he didn't know it came from the swallow, he didn't know it came from the Happy Prince, but he knew that with it he could buy all the firewood he needed, and finish his play.

The swallow flew back to the prince, "Dear Prince, I have done what you wanted. But tomorrow I must fly south. It is getting too cold for me now."

With that the swallow pulled his wing over his head and began to drop off to sleep. However, very soon he felt the same old DRIP, DRIP, DRIP. He tried to ignore it but again he felt DRIP, DRIP, DRIP on his head. Eventually and reluctantly he looked up at the prince and shouted, "Prince, I don't care what's wrong. I'm not helping."

With that he pulled his wing back over his head, but the tears continued: DRIP, DRIP, DRIP, DRIP, DRIP, DRIP. Eventually the swallow looked up. "OK, Prince, tell me what's wrong. But I'm not going to help." And so the prince began to explain.

"Today, dear Swallow, I looked over the city and I saw a little girl selling matches in the marketplace. She goes there every day to sell her matches. She's an orphan and has no one to look after her, so every night she sleeps on someone's doorstep and every day she sells her matches to get enough money to buy food and to buy more matches. But today she dropped all her matches into the water and now she has no matches to sell and she is trying to sleep, but she is very hungry."

The swallow was very upset to hear this tale and although he knew that he should be flying south, he offered to help the prince just one more time. "Hop onto my shoulder again, dear Swallow, and take my remaining sapphire eye to the little girl," the prince instructed. The swallow really didn't want to take the prince's last eye, but the prince was insistent so he took the eye and flew to the little girl. She was asleep, so the swallow placed the sapphire gently in the little girl's hand. When she woke up the little girl was so excited. She could now buy food and more matches, and even get somewhere to live. But she didn't know where the gift had come from. She didn't know it came from the swallow, she didn't know it came from the prince.

The swallow flew back to the prince and said: "Prince, now you have no eyes and you cannot see the city. Now, dear Prince, I will never leave you. I will stay and be your eyes forever."

"Then, Swallow, fly over all the city and come back and tell me what you see," said the prince.

The swallow set off and flew through the whole city, and then he came back and reported to the prince: "I have seen many rich people with fine clothes and lots of food living in fine homes."

The prince nodded. "Then fly again, Swallow, to the rest of the city and tell me what you see."

This time the swallow returned with a very different report. "I have seen many poor people who are hungry and have nowhere to live and who are dressed in rags."

The prince sighed and said to the swallow: "Swallow, my body is covered with the finest gold. Will you take it off piece by piece and take the pieces to the people who need it?"

So the swallow set to work at once until everyone in the city had money to buy food and houses and warm clothes. But nobody ever knew where the gold came from. They didn't know about the swallow; they didn't know about the prince.

Then winter came. The swallow flew back to the prince one morning, and looking up into the prince's face he said, "Prince, it's getting cold now, far too cold for me. I will miss you, dear Prince." And with that the little bird died. And at the same time the lead heart inside the prince broke in two. And there they stayed, the prince with the broken heart and the dead bird, far above the city.

Then one day the Lord Mayor walked down the main street. "What a fine city," he thought. "Everyone has a nice house and plenty of food and they all wear such nice clothes." But he didn't know of the swallow or the prince.

Then the Lord Mayor arrived at the statue of the prince and he was not impressed: "Look at that statue, so old and green and mouldy. I'm sure that used to be a nice statue… And what's that? It looks like there's a dead bird up there. We must build a new statue. A glorious statue, a statue of… well, me!"

So the Lord Mayor ordered the statue to be pulled down. Workmen came with hammers and smashed it into little pieces until there was hardly anything left. Then a workman came to the Lord Mayor, and in his hands he held the lead heart of the prince and the dead swallow. "This is all that's left, Lord Mayor. What shall I do with them?"

The Lord Mayor found the objects disgusting. "Throw them onto the rubbish tip outside the city."

And that's where they lay until one day God was talking with one of his angels. "Go to the city and bring back the two most precious things you can find."

The angel left at once and began his search of the city. He searched and searched but he couldn't find anything. Eventually he went outside the city and found the rubbish tip. And from the rubbish tip he took the heart of the prince and a little dead swallow and flew back to God with them. God looked at the objects and said to the angel. "You have chosen very well. For the most precious things in the city are those who help others, even when no one says thank you."

With that, God touched the swallow and the bird flew into God's garden. And God commanded the prince to live there too. And so they spent all of eternity together, happy in God's glorious garden.

The Lies People Tell

James was eight and always in trouble. But he thought that by telling lies he could always get out of trouble. And sometimes it actually worked!

One day as she went out to the shops, James's mum shouted up the stairs, "James, you make sure you feed Spot before you go out."

"OK, Mum!" James replied.

But with the rush to get out and play football with his friends, James forgot to feed the dog. Later that day when his mum asked him why Spot's bowl looked so clean, James told a lie. He said, "Well, Mum, it's because I've been teaching Spot to do his own washing-up. As soon as he finished his food he must have put it in the washing-up bowl, washed it clean, dried it, and put it back on the floor."

The amazing thing is James's mother believed him. His lie had worked.

James became even more convinced that it didn't matter how much trouble he was in, a lie would always get him out of trouble. But one lie doesn't usually mean the end. It usually leads to lots of other lies and then you can end up really trapped in them. James didn't believe that, but he was about to find out that it was true.

Hanging on Every Word

One day James got up really early. It was his birthday and what James wanted more than anything else was a new football. The last one had gone flat and when Dad had tried to fix it, it had exploded. James rushed downstairs, and there at the bottom of the stairs was his birthday present. He knew it was his football because of the shape. He pulled the wrapping paper off quickly. Eventually the ball was free.

"Happy Birthday," said James's dad. "I hope you like your new ball." But he added quickly, "But remember, you mustn't go to the park with it unless I take you. That road is too busy for you to cross alone. And if you cross that road without me, James, I will take the ball off you. Is that clear?"

James nodded.

The first thing James did was to write his name on the ball, and then he went out to play. He stood kicking the ball against the fence for a while, but that got very tiresome. He tried playing volleys and headers but that was no fun if nobody was watching him. James looked across the road. There, playing in the park, were all his friends. They waved. James looked around the garden. He looked towards the house. There was no sign of his dad anywhere. And so he crept across the road and started playing football with his friends, using his new ball.

That night when he came home, his dad asked him, "James, where have you been playing?"

James shrugged his shoulders and replied, "Out in the garden, of course."

"And you haven't been across the road and in the park?"

"No, Dad," James lied, "I've been in the garden."

"But Mrs Jones phoned me and said you were in the park," continued Dad.

"No, Dad," James continued to lie. "She must have been mistaken."

James's dad said no more. But the following day, James went back across the road to play with his football and his friends. He had a great time; he scored three goals, tackled everyone, and played the best he had ever played.

But that night his dad asked him again, "James, where have you been playing?"

James shrugged his shoulders and replied, "Out in the garden, of course."

"You haven't been across the road and in the park?" James's dad asked.

"No, Dad," James lied. "I've been in the garden."

"But Mrs Jones came round to tell me you were in the park."

"No, Dad," James continued to lie. "She must have been mistaken."

"But I checked in the garden and I couldn't see you anywhere."

James smiled, "I was hiding up the tree, Dad. I was going to jump out on you, but you went back in too fast."

Dad wasn't convinced, but he said no more.

The following day, James went back across the road to play with his football and his friends. He didn't have such a great time. His team lost. And James kicked his ball over Mrs Jones's fence.

That night his dad asked him again, "James, where have you been playing?"

James shrugged his shoulders and replied, "Out in the garden, of course."

"You haven't been across the road and in the park?" James's dad asked.

"No, Dad," James lied. "I've been in the garden."

"But Mrs Jones came round to tell me you were in the park," continued Dad.

"No, Dad," James continued to lie. "She must have been mistaken."

Then Dad pulled out the ball. "But she brought me this ball, James. She said you kicked this ball over her fence."

James began to sweat. "It just looks like mine, Dad. But mine is outside."

"But it has 'James' written on it. Still, if it's not yours, then I'll take this to the police station later as lost property."

What was James to do? He was trapped. The lies had trapped him. James was going to lose his ball. His new birthday ball. He was very worried. He liked his ball very much. James stood thinking for some time. Then, just as James's dad got to the front door, James shouted, "Dad, it was me! I was over in the park. It's my ball. It was me. I'm sorry."

James's dad turned around and smiled. He knew that James had lied and was glad that he had decided to tell the truth. James got his ball back. He was also grounded for three weeks. But he got his ball back.

Lies trap us.

Truth sets us free.

William Booth

He came up Mile End Road, East London, as the saffron light of evening flooded the sky, a tall, black-bearded man in a dark coat and wide-brimmed hat. He was walking quickly. He stopped outside a pub called The Blind Beggar. He drew an old Bible from his pocket and began to read out loud. The man was over six feet tall and the passers-by soon stopped to stare at this stranger with his unusual Midlands accent. People were drawn to listen. The man continued to speak in his "sing-song" voice, and there was something else that could clearly be detected through the accent: this man sincerely cared for people.

He continued to speak to the gathering multitude about how much God loved them. Then suddenly men came out of the pub and began to make fun of him. One threw an egg that broke on the man's cheek. The man calmly wiped the yoke away, bowed his head and prayed. Then he turned and continued on his way. Long he had thought about where God wanted him to go, and what God wanted him to do. He had dreamt of a journey to a far away jungle with strange inhabitants. But God had a different idea, and on this special night the man, William Booth, the Salvation Army's first general, walked through a human jungle, a city of over three million people.

He walked on, passing children as young as five who staggered about blind drunk. He watched fight after fight as man turned against man in a desire to conquer the other. He looked into the squalid houses where the sick, the dying, and very often the dead lay side by side on the cold floors. He walked on past tramps and homeless men, women, and children. He walked avoiding the countless drunks who had spent the precious pennies they had earned on drink, while their families sat hungry at home, the children desperate for food.

Eventually, around midnight, he placed a key in his front door. He turned it and entered. There sat his wife. She would not sleep until her beloved William returned. He stared at her, his grey eyes piercing.

"Tonight, darling," he announced, "I found my destiny."

The route that William Booth had taken on that first night was not unusual for him. He would often go to the most needy. He would often go to those who were drunk and desperate. And he would often stand outside The Blind Beggar pub and tell the people about Jesus.

One day, he stood in his usual position staring at a group of men who looked as if they had been drinking all day long. It was on this occasion that William first met Peter Monk. Peter approached William and asked him what he was doing. William responded, "I am looking for work."

Peter thought that William needed money, so he reached into his pocket to hand him some, but William waved him away and said: "I don't need money, sir. Over there, those men are my work. Men forgotten by man and God."

Peter Monk was puzzled by these strange comments, but he agreed with one thing.

"You are right, sir, these men are forgotten by God and man, and if you can do anything for them, it would be a great work."

"Well, I'm preaching tonight in the tent on the corner. You can come and bring a few of these people with you," replied William.

Peter nodded. He didn't know why, but he had agreed to attend. Williams knew very little about Peter Monk. He probably didn't know that Peter was a prize fighter. Peter would fight other men for money. The fight usually took place behind The Blind Beggar.

Peter had agreed to go to the tent to listen to William, but before he could go, he had a fight. Peter made his way to the usual place and stripped off his top. He watched as men bet money on who would win, and he watched as his opponent took off his top and got ready to fight. They exchanged looks, walked towards each other, and began to fight. It was a ferocious fight. There was much damage to both men's faces and it looked as if it could last for many hours. Then Peter Monk brought it to a conclusion with a combination of dazzling blows to his opponent's body and a cracking finisher to his jaw. Peter's friends cheered and collected their money.

Peter was cut badly, but remembered his promise to go to listen to William. He put on his shirt and jacket and went to find the tent. When he arrived, he was surprised by the sight. William was standing at the front trying to speak while some local troublemakers were yelling insults and throwing things. There was no way William could be heard. Peter remembered that William wanted to help people like these and decided to help him. Peter took off his jacket and went and stood beside William with his arms folded. Peter was a very tough man, and the cuts and fresh blood on his face just made him look even tougher. A hush fell over the crowd and the troublemakers sat down to listen.

William spoke to them about how much God loved them. Within a few days, Peter Monk had given up fighting and decided that he too would give his life to helping people and telling them about the love of Jesus, just like William Booth. And with men like

Peter Monk and with the help of his wife, Catherine, William began to form an army of people who would help others and tell them about the love of Jesus.

And today this international church works in over a hundred countries across the world. They still offer help to people who are hungry, poor, homeless, or, who are in need in some other way. So it is that the Salvation Army continues to fulfil William Booth's vision to share God's love with everyone.

Oliver and Zoë

"Hello, bright sun!" shouted Oliver. "Hello, little clouds." Oliver couldn't remember a time when he had felt so happy.

He was out in the meadow flying his kite.

And then he saw it. The sight that was to ruin his day.

There, on the other side of the hedge, his five-year-old sister, Zoë, was giving his mother a daffodil and in return his mother gave Zoë a big hug.

Suddenly it seemed to Oliver as if a dark cloud had crept into the sky. Zoë seemed to be getting a lot of hugs lately. He hadn't really been keeping count, but he was sure she was getting more hugs than him.

"She's stealing all the love," he said to himself. "Soon there won't be any left for me." So he decided he'd be a dark cloud in Zoë's day.

"Guess what," Oliver said to Zoë as soon as his mother had gone. "Mum loves me the best!"

Zoë's face turned red. "No, she doesn't. She loves us the same."

"Poor Zoë," sighed Oliver. "I wish Mum could have two favourites, but favourite means one and one means me."

Zoë was getting very cross and then she had an idea.

"Why don't we have a contest?" Zoë said. "Whoever gets the most hugs and kisses from Mum before supper-time will be the winner."

Oliver wasn't sure he was going to win, but he really had no choice now. "Well, all right."

Zoë rushed into the house to win her first kiss.

"I'll do the dusting for you, Mum. You sit down and rest your feet."

Mum gave Zoë a delighted kiss. "You are very thoughtful, Zoë."

"I can do better than that." Oliver told himself. "I'll make Mum a soothing footbath."

And he made his way to the bathroom to find the right ingredients.

He mixed some pink bubble bath with some orange bubble bath and some blue bubble bath. He added some of his own special green bubble bath from his Thunderbirds holder. He put in some bath salts and then added some bits and pieces he found in the cabinet under the sink. He then added the hot water. The steam started to swirl up into the air and – rather unusually, Oliver thought – the water had turned green. He carried the bowl downstairs.

His mum seemed delighted and he was sure he would get many hugs and kisses for this. Mum took off her shoes and socks and placed her feet into the bowl. All seemed fine. Mum looked very relaxed. Then suddenly her feet began to burn. She gave a scream and kicked out. The bowl fell over and spilt green gunge all over the carpet. What was worse, Mum's legs and feet had gone green. She looked like the Incredible Hulk and she was not happy.

Oliver ran for it, out through the garden door and into the garden.

With a heavy heart, Oliver walked up and down the garden wondering what he could try next. Then, to his astonishment, he heard music coming from the house. He gazed in through the living room window to see his sister, the hug thief, playing piano for Mum.

If Zoë was going to play the piano, Oliver was going to do something even more wonderful. He was going to make Mum his own amazing music box.

He got to work at once. He went to the shed to collect an old box, some glue and some paint. He then put the box together, finishing it off with a lovely coat of purple paint. There was just one thing missing – the music. But Oliver had an idea for this. He spent the next two hours rummaging around in the grass near his house until he had collected twenty or so grasshoppers. He then placed them in his box and closed the lid.

The grasshoppers hopped around and rubbed their legs together making the click, click sound that grasshoppers make. Oliver thought it sounded like wonderful music and took it into his mum. This time he was going to win. He was sure to get many hugs and kisses for this one.

He walked into the house. "Sorry about earlier, Mum," he said, "but look what I've done for you." And with that, he pulled out his music box. Mum was impressed, but just as Oliver was passing the box to his mum, the bottom fell out and twenty or so very angry grasshoppers started to jump all over the house. Oliver scurried around trying to catch them, while his mum screamed and jumped on a chair. Oliver knew it was no good and ran back into the garden.

Oliver flopped on the ground underneath one of the trees. "Not a single hug all day," he mumbled to himself.

He gazed up into the sky. It had seemed such a nice day. And now it was ruined.

But what was this above his head, in the tree? Of course, apples. He would take his mum some apples.

He went to the shed and collected the ladder. It was quite an old ladder, but Oliver wasn't very heavy and he was sure he would be able to safely reach the apples. He positioned the ladder in front of the tree and began to climb. He went up five steps, but just as he put his foot on the sixth step, the step snapped. But he was fine, he just fell back one step. He stepped over step six and began to climb higher and higher. He was nearly there. One more step and he was there. He began to gather apples and put them in his pockets. Five apples, six apples, seven apples, then… Snap!

The top step broke and Oliver came tumbling down. The apples lay on the ground, squashed, and next to the apples lay a very squashed Oliver. He began to cry loudly. Their neighbour, Edmund, saw the whole thing and rushed around to help Oliver. After checking to see if anything was broken, he picked up the little boy and carried him quickly into the house.

"Nothing too serious," called Edmund as he came in. "Just a lot of bruises and scrapes."

In seconds, Mum had ice packs and a blanket and bowl of soup for her poor wounded boy. Oliver was getting more hugs and kisses than Zoë could count.

"Oliver really is your favourite!" Zoë began to cry.

Mum looked confused.

"All day long Oliver has messed everything up. He ruined the carpet, he turned your feet green, he let bugs run free in the house, and he fell out of a tree. And he still gets all the love."

Mum picked Zoë up and rested her on her knee, right next to Oliver.

"Zoë," Mum began, "you are my favourite Zoë and Oliver is my favourite Oliver. I don't love you because of what you do for me. I love you because you're my children."

Then she gave them both a special hug.

That night, as Zoë and Oliver were lying in their bunk beds, Zoë said, "I'm glad Mum loves us both the same. It would be sad if she only loved one of us."

"Yes, it would," Oliver answered.

The silvery moon shone into the room as the stars twinkled against the dark sky. Zoë was just drifting off to sleep when Oliver added: "Too bad Dad loves me best."

Fig Leaf Phil

Captain Philip Anthony Luke John Hogwash had been captain of the *Jolly Jim* for the last ten years. He had sailed the seven seas. He had carried prime ministers and kings, he had carried dukes and earls and princesses and presidents. He had gathered buried treasure and even discovered some countries that had never been visited before. But right now Captain Phil was in trouble. He was in the most serious storm of his entire life and he was alone. His crew had been in a rowing boat visiting a nearby harbour when the storm had blown up – seemingly from nowhere – and the anchor had broken and the ship had been swept out to sea. Captain Phil had battled hard to steer the ship in some sort of direction, but by himself it was impossible. The rain hammered down on him, the wind seemed determined to throw him overboard, and eventually he had given up. The ship was being pulled by the wind towards who knew where.

There was a bright flash and then a crack. Lightning had struck the mainsail and the mast was toppling towards the ship below. Captain Phil tried to jump aside but he was too slow. His legs were trapped under the mast. The ship was heading for some rocks and Captain Phil was stuck. The ship looked as if it would sink and take

Captain Phil with it. He had to do something. He pulled out his dagger and began to cut off his lovely leather shoes. Amazingly, he managed to slide his feet out.

The ship was getting closer to the rocks. Captain Philip stood on the edge of the deck. The rain continued to hammer down. The wind howled, and eventually it happened – the ship hit the rocks.

Captain Phil was thrown to the edge rail and stared into the water below. He had to jump. If he didn't, he would go down with the ship. He had to take a risk. If he jumped into the water he may hurt himself. If he didn't, he was sure to drown. So Captain Phil jumped. He hit the water very hard. The waves threw him towards an island, where he rolled onto the beach. He was very wet and very cold. His clothes were ripped to shreds and his arm had a nasty gash. But he was alive.

Phil lay on the beach trying to catch his breath. Waves still lapped over his body. His trousers were now torn shorts and his shirt had no buttons left. He wondered where he was. He tried to sit up, but his body was still very battered and bruised. Then he heard some screaming. He turned his head slowly, so as not to attract attention. He could just about make out several men chasing a young woman across the beach. The woman wore a jewelled skirt and a brightly coloured top. The men who were chasing her wore sandy-coloured clothes and round hunter's hats on their heads. Each man carried a gun, but nobody was shooting. They obviously wanted to catch this woman alive. Phil looked on with horror as one of the men threw a net towards the woman, who tripped over and was captured. More men then came, not as well-dressed as the first ones but certainly not wearing rags. Phil guessed that they must be the men's servants. The men quickly took the net off the woman and pushed her roughly into a wooden cage. The servants then picked up the cage and set off.

Phil dragged himself to his feet and set off to follow the young woman. His bones ached, his muscles hurt, but he was determined to find out where they were taking her. He dragged himself through thick jungle, twisting his ankle and adding to the pain in the process. He narrowly escaped being bitten by what was clearly a very poisonous snake that the hunters had disturbed, and as night-time fell he only just stopped himself from falling over a cliff edge that he hadn't seen. But still he followed.

As the darkness began to grip the island, the men came to a camp. A high bamboo fence surrounded it and the gate that marked the entrance was guarded by more of the men's servants. Phil watched from his hiding place, wondering what he should do. If he went down to that camp he could be caught; he had already been through a whole range of dangers to get here in the first place. What a day he was having – shipwrecked, and now about to risk his life again to save a woman he had never met.

Phil waited until all was quiet, and then he made his way down to the camp. Slowly and methodically he began to dig his way under the bamboo until there was a hole big enough for him to drag himself through. He hid in the shadows, moving very slowly and very stealthily for a man with so many bruises. He caught sight of the woman and couldn't believe it. She was tied up but completely unguarded. He crept over. She turned her head and was about to scream when Phil lifted his finger to his lips and said, "I've come to save you. Be quiet or we will both die."

She obeyed. She didn't know who he was, but he seemed to be her only chance. Slowly, very slowly, the ropes were untied and the pair began to creep back towards the hole. Phil couldn't believe how easy it had been. But as he was lowering the woman into the hole, he heard an enormous bang! and pieces of the bamboo fence nearby splintered off. Blood was oozing from his shoulder. Phil had been shot, but it wasn't a serious wound. He dropped into the hole and climbed quickly up the other side. By now, the camp was a buzz of activity; all the lights were on, all the men were out and the gates were open. Phil knew the men would search all night if necessary.

Phil and the woman ran into the jungle as fast as they could. They ran and ran until they could run no further, then they climbed the tallest tree they could find and sat still. It wasn't long before the men came along. They stopped below Phil's tree and looked around. They stood there for what seemed like an eternity, but eventually they walked on. Phil and the woman sat on a branch of the tree, shaking.

Phil looked at her. 'What's your name, and why did those men take you?'

"My name is Tuesday," she responded. "Princess Tuesday. And the men wanted to capture me because I know the secret."

Phil was too tired to ask what the secret was. His shoulder was leaking blood. His bones were aching, he had bruises on his bruises. He was on an island with Princess Tuesday who knew the secret, with men dressed in camouflage, and his ship was at the bottom of the ocean.

His mind was swirling, his thoughts overloading. He passed out and fell out of the tree.

When Phil next opened his eyes, he was looking up into the face of Princess Tuesday. She was mopping his brow with a damp cloth and speaking to him very softly. The memory of the night before came rushing back to him. He jumped up quickly and wished he hadn't. He was left holding his spinning head.

When Phil began to focus, he realized that there was somebody with Princess Tuesday. "

"Who are you?" Phil enquired, surprised by how strong his voice was sounding.

The man was quite short, with a tummy that hung over his tight trousers. He answered, "I am Shalam. I am a friend of the king and of Princess Tuesday. I have come to help you bring the princess back home."

Phil listened and then stood up and shook hands with Shalam.

"Well, I have no idea where the princess lives or how to get there, but we had better get going before those hunter people come back."

The three walked for what seemed like hours, but all the time Shalam kept whispering to Phil, "We can't trust the princess. She will lead us into a trap. She is tired. She has been under much stress, and being captured has affected her. The princess, she is very confused."

Flies buzzed around their heads and the sun beat down on them. Phil was feeling very uncomfortable, but they kept walking. He figured they must be heading towards the palace where the princess lived. He would never have guessed that the island was as big as it was. They came to a point in the path where it branched into two different directions.

"Which way now?" asked Phil.

But Princess Tuesday and Shalam seemed to have different ideas about which way they should go. They began to shout, then to argue. Princess Tuesday shouted, "Shalam, why do you want us to go down that way? You know it's dangerous. It is longer, and the hunters go there."

Shalam yelled back, "You see, Fig Leaf Phil?" for that is what Shalam called Phil on account of his ripped clothes. "She does not know what she is saying."

Phil looked from one to the other: from Princess Tuesday to Shalam. How was he to decide? He looked at the princess, but he remembered the words of Shalam in the back of his mind: "She is tired. She has been under much stress."

Phil grabbed the Princess's arm and dragged her in the direction that Shalam had indicated.

"You have chosen well, Phil," Shalam mumbled.

But as they turned the corner, hunters surrounded them. They seemed to come from all directions, pushing from behind the trees and the bushes. All with guns aimed at Phil, the princess, and Shalam.

"Well, Shalam," Phil said. "We have ended up trapped."

Shalam began to laugh. Then he walked away from Phil and Princess Tuesday, and joined the hunters. He pulled a round hat out of his bag and placed it on his head.

"Phil, you are so easily led. Let me introduce you to my friends." Then, turning his attention to Princess Tuesday, he whispered, "and tomorrow, Princess, you and your secret will die."

Phil couldn't believe it. How could he have been so stupid? He had believed Shalam when he knew nothing about him. He had been completely fooled. It had looked as if Shalam would be his friend, but now it was clear he was not. But Phil would have much time to think about these things. He was about to spend the night trapped in a bamboo cage with Princess Tuesday.

As daybreak arrived, he realized that the bamboo cage was moving. Men were carrying the cage! He could just make out the shape of the palace in the distance. He shook Princess Tuesday gently by the shoulder until she woke up.

"Princess, look! They're taking us to the palace. Now everything's going to be fine. Your dad is going to set us free and then I can find a ship off this island."

Princess Tuesday began to shake her head slowly, "No, Phil. That's what the secret is. The king is not the king."

Phil was confused, but Princess Tuesday explained: "My father has an identical twin brother, and he is pretending to be my father and convincing people that he is really the king – but he is no king. He is the leader of the hunters, and now he wants to take over the whole kingdom. I'd never have worked it out, but my dad has a scar on the back of his leg and when I saw the impostor king in the swimming pool last week there was no scar. He saw me staring, and he knew that I'd worked it out. That's why I ran away and that's why the hunters were trying to catch me."

Phil listened patiently. Eventually the hunters arrived at the palace, and Shalam commanded the men carrying the bamboo cage to go around the back and into the royal gardens. When the cage was eventually laid to rest, the impostor king was there to greet them. "Hello, Princess, and hello, Captain. Don't look so surprised. I saw your ship go down, and if you hadn't been in such a rush to rescue the princess then I would have happily helped you get to another ship. As it is, you know too much."

Phil was about to argue, but there was nothing he could think of saying. He knew he was in a lot of trouble.

The impostor king simply smiled and commanded the guards to throw them into prison. The order was given, and Phil was grabbed and taken into the palace. The next thing he was aware of was sliding down a tube and smashing onto the hard floor of the underground prison. Seconds later there was another crash, and he guessed that Princess Tuesday had landed next to him.

When his eyes eventually became used to the dim light, he saw he was in a damp concrete room. In the distance he could see tiny scuttling animals in the distance that he guessed were rats. And propped up in a corner, wrapped in a blanket, was undoubtedly the shape of a man – a very thin man. Princess Tuesday had obviously been observing the same scene for she suddenly cried, "Father!" and scrambled over to the man. Phil followed her, but kept his distance as he listened to the sobs from the princess: "Father, what have they done to you? Father, what have they done?"

They may have found the king, but they were still trapped and the impostor king was ruining the kingdom. They stared up at the hole they had just fallen through. Surely there was no way up? But it was worth a try. Phil carefully stood on the king's shoulders and stretched back up to the tube he had plummeted through only a short time before. He crawled into the tube and slowly began to make his way back up it. Eventually he reached the top. He found himself in a dark room, but there was a door – he opened it quietly and began to walk down the corridor. He could hear a lot of noise. He had reached the main hall. There seemed to be some sort of ceremony taking place. It looked as if half the kingdom had gathered. Phil suddenly noticed some stairs towards the back of the hall, leading downwards. He crept down the long winding staircase while everyone was distracted by the ceremony. There were no guards anywhere to be seen. Phil guessed they must all be upstairs.

Just when Phil thought that it couldn't get any easier, he arrived outside the cell where the princess and the king were held, only to discover there was a simple bolt on the outside. Phil pulled back the bolt and they were free, all of them. They began to make their way back upstairs and into the hall. The plan had been to sneak straight out of the main gate, but just as they were about to escape, Phil clumsily knocked over an enormous vase just as the impostor king had stood to speak and everyone had gone very quiet. Everybody turned and stared, and then the impostor king gave the order: "Arrest that man! He is a spy."

The guards had just grabbed Phil when the real king stepped forward and proclaimed: "Not so fast. Let him go." He pointed to the impostor. "And that man is not the real king. I am."

A deathly hush fell over the whole palace. The Lord Chancellor stared at both men and then walked up to the impostor king and looked at his leg. He then walked over to the real king and looked at his. There could be no doubt; one bore the scar, the other didn't. The Lord Chancellor announced for all to hear, "We have been tricked. Arrest that pretend king! Throw him in prison."

The hunters were quick to respond. They had pulled out their guns and were ready to fight, but they were no match for the palace guard who quickly disarmed them, throwing them onto the ground to beg for mercy. It was all over and the good guys had most certainly won.

There was a party and a lot of celebrating. The impostor and the hunters were banished from the island and the kingdom returned to normal. Phil was a hero. Without him, the impostor king may have triumphed. The king instantly made him a knight and, of course, gave the princess permission to marry him. His ragged clothes were replaced by more fitting garments (although they were more brightly coloured than Phil would have liked).

To be a knight, to live on the desert island paradise for the rest of his life… To maybe marry the princess and live happily ever after among the palm trees and coconuts… To swim in the sea, to have anything he wanted… Everything seemed perfect. But Phil also knew that he was not supposed to live the rest of his life like that. He was a sea captain, an adventurer, a pioneer. He would never be happy sitting on the beach day after day. He had a job to do and he would do it. Maybe one day he would return, but for now, his job here was done and he longed to return to the sea.

Several weeks later, when the next ship was passing the island, Phil kissed Princess Tuesday goodbye. He then turned and swam out to the ship. He would be a captain again and in years to come he would return to the little island and marry the princess. But he had many adventures to get through before then.

Breakfast from Heaven

George Müller started working in Bristol in 1832. He was to be the leader of a church. But unlike many other jobs, this one didn't come with any money, nobody was paying him to preach, to teach the Bible, or to help people in need, so he had to trust God to provide for all the things he needed, whether food or clothes or a home. But George was an exceptional church leader and both the Gideon and Bethesda Chapels grew very quickly in numbers in a short time. By the time George completed his work there, 2,000 people were coming to his church every week.

At the age of seventy, George began to make great evangelistic tours. He travelled 200,000 miles, going around the world and preaching in many lands and in several different languages. He frequently spoke to as many as 4,500 or 5,000 persons. Three times he preached throughout the length and breadth of the United States. He continued his missionary or evangelistic tours until he was ninety years of age. It is estimated that he spoke to nearly three million people in his services.

But George felt that his greatest achievement was not the large church or the huge numbers he talked to, or the many countries he visited, but instead it was the building of the great orphanages in Bristol. These began with one house which provided a home for thirty girls. But eventually thousands of boys and girls were housed in specially made buildings. From the beginning, George decided to trust God, just as he had always done. Most days went like this:

"Children," said George, "it will soon be time for school, so let's pray: Dear Father, thank you for what we are going to eat."

The orphanages were for very poor children. Children who nobody wanted and nobody would look after. George didn't receive any money from the government to run his orphanage, and he didn't receive any money from other people. He just trusted God. And this was another morning in the orphanage when they were trusting God. There was no food. The children were hungry. It was time to eat breakfast. But Müller trusted God. He had prayed, so the food would certainly come.

Just then a knock sounded at the door, and there stood the local baker. "Mr Müller," he said, "I couldn't sleep last night. Somehow I felt you didn't have bread for breakfast, and the Lord wanted me to send you some. So I have been up since two o'clock this morning and baked some fresh bread for you."

Müller thanked the baker and praised God for his care. "Children," he announced, "not only do we have bread this morning, but it is fresh bread."

Right away there came a second knock at the door. This time it was the milkman. "My cart has broken down outside the orphanage, and I must empty it before it can be fixed. Do the children need some milk?"

So the children ate their fresh bread and drank their fresh milk. Every meal time the children and George Müller prayed, and every meal time God provided.

George started the orphanage with just a handful of coins in his pocket; but he prayed and God began to tell people to send money to George. He built the buildings and and fed the children. He was in charge for the next sixty years. But every day he trusted God. And never did God let him down.

An amazing life, lived by a man who simply trusted God.

The Watchman

Alexander was a mighty warrior who had yet to lose a battle, that's how he came to be called Alexander the Great. The next day there was going to be an important battle, and Alexander knew that his armies were in need of a rest. The Persians were camped nearby and there was a sense of great unease in the camp. Alexander knew that his men were very vulnerable as they slept. There was nothing to stop the Persians from creeping into the camp and wiping out hundreds of Alexander's soldiers. They might even kill Alexander himself.

To protect the army, Alexander came up with the idea of using watchmen. He made the 35,000 soldiers sleep in a large circle, and at regular intervals around the circumference of the circle he placed a watchman. The watchman's job was very simple. He was to keep watch and if he saw the enemy approaching he was to blow his trumpet.

The soldiers didn't like taking their turn as watchmen. It would mean a long night of standing and looking out into the darkness. One of the soldiers on this particular night really hated it. He had marched all day long and hadn't slept very well the previous night. And now he was standing in the cold night air, waiting and watching. His eyelids were very heavy. He would have loved to be asleep but he knew that instead he needed to stand and watch.

When 10 p.m. came, the camp was quiet except for one or two soldiers chatting. The soldier felt so tired but kept watch.

By 11 p.m. he was feeling very sleepy, but he leaned against a nearby tree and kept watching.

Midnight came, and the camp was totally silent, with only the sound of snoring in the distance. The soldier felt very, very tired. He sat down, still leaning against that tree.

At 2 a.m. the soldier's eyes began to close. He forced them open again, but he was so tired. It was getting cold now. He reached into his bag and wrapped a blanket around himself.

At 3 a.m., his eyes were nearly closed.

By 4 a.m., he was fast asleep, wrapped in the blanket and leaning against the tree.

At 5 a.m., the soldier felt a hand grab his throat. He felt himself being lifted off the ground and slammed against the tree with his legs dangling in the air. He was sure that when he opened his eyes he would look into the face of one of the Persians, and he felt for sure that any moment now a dagger would be pushed into his chest. But as he opened them, the sight which met his eyes was far more frightening to this soldier than any Persian. There, gazing up at him, holding him with one enormous arm, fingers clenching his throat, was Alexander the Great.

Alexander looked at the soldier, his eyes burning with anger, his fingers able to squeeze the life out of the man with ease: "What is your name soldier?" Alexander demanded.

Through his tight throat the soldier croaked: "Alexander, sir. My name is Alexander."

"What?"

"Alexander, sir. My mother named me after you."

Alexander looked at the soldier, then he let go of his grip. The soldier fell into a heap on the ground. Alexander looked down at him, and with venom in his voice said: "Soldier, either change the way you behave or change your name."

Lilly the
Mountain Lioness

"Listen to me, Lilly. You can go anywhere you want. Do anything you want. Most animals will run away from you, some will play with you, but all will respect you. You are a mountain lioness. You are very fierce."

Lilly listened. She liked the fact that she was the toughest of all the animals on this part of the mountain. Well, one of the toughest. Her mum – who was giving the talk – was tougher, and her cousins who shared the pride with her were also very fierce. Then, of course, there was Carro; he was the head of the pride and Lilly didn't know anyone who was even half as scary as him. He didn't talk to her much, even though he was her father. He just stood on a large rock watching over the pride. He was in charge.

Lilly's mum continued: "Play in the woods, chase the squirrels, frighten the rabbits, jump over the stream, climb the trees, do whatever you want, but don't wander into the open fields. The hunters set their traps there and will happily capture you and send you off to some zoo where you'll be caged up for the rest of your life. Don't go into the open fields."

Lilly listened patiently. She loved her mum very much, but she did go on sometimes. She was a little bit of a nag. But Lilly smiled politely and nodded. She heard the same talk every morning. She knew it word for word: "Don't go into the open fields."

Today it was sunny. It usually was. Lilly wandered out looking for something to do. She wandered over to the squirrels.

"Let's see if I can catch one of those," she thought to herself.

Lilly raced after the squirrels, but they all dodged her very quickly and ran up some trees. She tried climbing after them, but she couldn't get high enough. Lilly soon gave up.

"Maybe I'll go and catch a rabbit for my lunch."

But even though she looked around for almost an hour, not a single rabbit came out of its hole. She jumped over the stream a couple of times, she tried climbing some more trees, she frightened away some vultures who were looking for a snack, and eventually she lay in the sun. But she still wanted something a little bit more interesting to do.

She lay sunbathing for some time, until a butterfly came and landed on her nose. She snapped at the butterfly, but the butterfly flew off and landed on a nearby flower. Lilly jumped towards the butterfly, but again the butterfly easily avoided Lilly's jaws and moved to another flower a bit further away.

"At last," Lilly thought, "a decent challenge."

She leapt towards the butterfly again, and again the butterfly flew off. This time the butterfly kept flying, and Lilly ran behind, swinging her tail and trying desperately to catch the butterfly.

The game went on for some time, with Lilly pouncing and snapping her mouth and the butterfly dodging and gracefully flying. Eventually Lilly came to the edge of the open fields and stopped dead. She looked into the fields. She couldn't see anything or anyone, just wide open fields. And there in the middle of the field, the butterfly still flew, almost teasing Lilly into following.

Lilly the Mountain Lioness

Lilly hesitated at the edge of the field. She knew the rule: "Don't go into the open fields." But she saw the butterfly and couldn't resist it. She ran into the field and straight at the butterfly. She took one final leap at the butterfly and sailed through the air towards it, she opened her mouth, snapped it closed, but missed the butterfly. She prepared herself to land. She put her front paws down. But as she touched the ground, the ground gave way. She fell and fell, and then landed with a heavy bump. Where was she? She looked around. She was in a trap. A hunter's trap.

Lilly felt very sad as she sat there. Soon afterwards, the hunters came and were overjoyed at their catch. They hauled Lilly out of the hole and, although she tried to escape, they pushed her towards a small metal cage. This lioness would be worth lots of money to them when they took her home and sold her to the zoo. But then they heard a sound that made their very bones rattle. A sound that filled them with fear. A roar. The loudest roar they would ever hear, and there behind them stood Carro, king of the lions. His mouth wide open, his teeth bared, his mane flowing. They looked at their captured lioness, but no matter how much money they would get – she wasn't worth fighting Carro for. They knew that it wasn't a fight they could win. They ran expecting to feel Carro's enormous paws on their shoulders at any time, waiting for the bite that would kill them. They ran. But no paws, no bite. Carro did not give chase. Instead he looked at Lilly, who felt very ashamed. But Carro never said anything, he knew the lesson had been learnt. He turned and walked back towards his rock. Lilly ran behind him. She knew that her mum would be very cross. But she was happy to be alive and not in a zoo.

Ted the Toff

Ted the Toff was very, very posh, and very, very rich. He lived in a huge mansion at the edge of Green Acres. But he wasn't in his mansion today. He'd just bought a new business called Sparkly Springs, a huge lake in the middle of the loveliest countryside in the world. Sparkly Springs was very, very popular. Hundreds of people came to it every day. They ate in the café overlooking the lake. They bought pictures from the shop, and sat at the picnic tables and watched the swans swimming. Sparkly Springs made a lot of money every week from all the people that visited, but Ted the Toff was going to make even more. Or so he thought.

His first idea was to put all the prices up. But after looking in the café, and walking around the shop, he soon realized how impossible that would be. Then he thought about charging people to come in, but he didn't think that would be a very popular idea. Eventually he came up with another plan. He would get rid of some of the staff. There seemed to be too many anyway. He would save money by paying fewer people, and then he would become even richer.

The very next day he called each of the staff into his office in turn, and asked them to explain what they did.

"I'm Cathy. I'm the cleaning lady. I mop the café, and I clean your office."

"I'm Katy. I sell things in the shop."

"I'm Percy. I make sure all the cars are parked properly in the car park."

"I'm Kathleen, I cook things for the café."

Ted listened to fifteen different people explaining their jobs, and they all sounded incredibly important. He didn't think he'd be able to sack anyone. Until Larry walked in.

"I'm Larry. I collect the rubbish which is left near the lake."

"That's it," thought Ted, "I'll put up a sign saying:

PLEASE TAKE
YOUR
RUBBISH HOME

"Then I can sack Larry."

That's what Ted did. He put up the sign and sacked Larry. But it didn't work out as he'd planned. The next week everything seemed to go well. Most people took their rubbish home. One or two people forgot, but that wasn't so bad. Ted saw a couple of old crisp bags at the side of the lake, but nothing much, really. The following week was the same, and the week after that. Ted noticed that often little bits of rubbish blew into the lake, but he didn't think it mattered. He was so pleased with himself; he was becoming richer and richer every week.

But the lake had started to change. A small stream flowed into it, and a small stream flowed out the other side. But slowly the way out of the lake was becoming blocked because of the bags and other bits. So the water had nowhere to go, and the rubbish began to pile up. After another six months, the lake started to smell. It smelt disgusting. The people stopped coming to the lake. They started going elsewhere. Ted was losing lots and lots of money, and he didn't understand what was going on. In the end, he was so upset that he called all the staff together and asked them: "What's going on? Why is the lake smelly?"

All the staff agreed: "It's because you sacked Larry. Larry did an important job."

"No, he didn't," Ted protested. "He just picked up the odd crisp bag every now and then. He hardly did anything."

The staff explained to Ted: "It all builds up. A little today and a little tomorrow and a little the next day and before long the lake is blocked and begins to smell. Our hearts are the same," they said. "They don't get full of bad things straight away, but if we keep doing bad things and we never ask God to forgive us and take the bad things away, eventually our hearts are full of rotten, horrible things."

Ted hated to admit he was wrong, but he hated to lose money even more.

"Where is Larry?" he shouted. "Bring me Larry."

Eventually Larry was found and agreed to come back to work, as long as Ted paid him twice as much as before.

Within a month everything was back to normal and all the people started to come back. The only thing that had changed was Larry now had much more money!

Kevin Runs Away

Kevin really was having a rough time. He'd been grounded for two whole months, for stealing from the shops. And now, with only a day to go before he could finally go back out to play, disaster had struck.

It was an accident – a real accident, for a change. He had seen this tiny fly on the windowsill. It was annoying him. He'd taken a rolled up newspaper and tried to splat it. But that sneaky old fly had taken off as the newspaper came closer and he'd missed and knocked over a vase. He'd dived to try to catch the vase and missed, knocking it into another vase. They'd both smashed. And Kevin knew that they were worth lots of money.

"I'm going to get grounded for a year," he moaned, "or maybe even longer. Why didn't I watch what I was doing?"

Kevin hated being grounded. He hated having to stay in the house while all his friends were outside playing. He could see them through the window, having a great time. He was very sad. He'd taken his punishment. He'd stayed in for two months and now, because of a little accident, he was going to get grounded for a year.

"Why do Mum and Dad hate me?" he thought. "I'm going to run away to the mountain. I'm not staying here a moment longer.

They just want to punish me all the time."

Kevin opened his front door and off he ran. He was going to run as far away as he could. He wasn't going to stay at home a moment longer with parents who were going to punish him all the time.

He ran for quite some time. Eventually he came to a part of the mountain he had never been to before. He kept going. But before long, he knew that he was completely lost. He curled up in some nearby ferns and tried to sleep. He heard every crack of branches, every whistle of the wind, every hoot of an owl, but eventually he slept, only to be woken minutes later – well, it felt like minutes, but now the sun was up – by a shepherd. Kevin was stiff and damp from the morning dew.

The shepherd smiled and asked, "Why are you here, Kevin? The mountain can be dangerous and sometimes very cold."

"Because my mum and dad like to punish me for things I didn't mean to do. And they ground me for months."

Again the shepherd smiled. "I'm not sure that's true, Kevin. I'm not sure they would punish you for breaking things by accident. Maybe for stealing, but not for accidents."

Kevin was getting a little worried. How did this shepherd know about that? And now he thought about it, how did he know his name? Kevin asked nervously, "Can you take me home?"

"Of course," replied the shepherd. The shepherd walked Kevin back down the mountain and to the top of the street where the mountain ended. "I can go no further."

Kevin ran down the street to his house. Kevin's mum was stood at the door. She took one look at Kevin and burst into floods of tears: she had been so worried. "Sorry for breaking the vase." he blurted out. "It was an accident."

"Thank you for apologizing, but we were much more worried about you than about those foolish old vases."

"So I'm not grounded, then?" asked Kevin.

"Of course not. We don't like grounding you, but when you deliberately do things wrong we have to. Kevin, we love you."

Kevin was happy to be home, and soon he would be allowed to play with his friends again.

"But one more thing," Kevin's mum said. "How did you get home? We have search parties out looking for you."

"The shepherd brought me."

"Oh," replied Mum, but she didn't say any more in case she frightened Kevin, for she knew that there hadn't been a shepherd on these mountains for over a hundred years.

Tommy Thomas, Jedi Knight

Tommy Thomas was eleven years old. That meant he was in Mr Harris's class. He was "average" – well, that's what all his school reports said:

Games	**Tommy is average**
English	**Tommy is average**
Maths	**Tommy is average**
Science	**Tommy is average**

Tommy was average height, he had average-colour, mousy hair, he wore average clothes, he wasn't particularly cool, and he wasn't the class leader – that job went to Gordon; everyone loved Gordon. He wasn't the class joker, that job went to Jason – he was just so funny. Tommy just sat in the class with the rest and was… well… average. He sat on the same table as Susan, Anna, and Chris. Susan and Anna were smart, they were always working very hard. Chris was into dinosaurs. He would draw lots of different dinosaurs; he would draw T-Rexes, pterodactyls and brontosauruses; Tommy would just sit there, and dream…

In his dreams he was a hero dressed in white, he held his light sabre high and proud, bullies ran away from him, and everyone loved him and wanted his autograph. He was Tommy Thomas, Jedi Knight. Fearless fighter for light and truth, constantly rescuing the beautiful princess who had been captured by the evil Darth Mr Harris. The princess was always Anna. Tommy liked Anna. And so he spent most of his days dreaming. Dreaming of being a hero. Dreaming of being Tommy Thomas, Jedi Knight.

That's what he was doing right now. He was just pushing Darth Mr Harris to the ground with his fluorescent green light sabre, just about to untie Princess Anna when…

BANG!

Mr Harris's ruler fell hard onto the desk. Tommy almost jumped out of his skin.

"Tommy! What is eight times seven?"

Tommy hadn't been paying attention, he was miles away.

"Ah – it's, it's, it's a really big number, sir!"

The class giggled. Mr Harris didn't giggle. He walked towards Tommy with his ruler in his hand.

"Fifty-six," whispered Anna. "The answer's fifty-six."

"Fifty-six," shouted Tommy "The answer is fifty-six."

Mr Harris stopped and smiled. "So you were listening." He walked back to the front. Thomas smiled at Anna. She looked away.

Tommy hated Fridays. He liked the fact that it was the last day of school, but that meant field games. In the winter they played hockey. Tommy hated hockey. But in the summer it was even worse – it was athletics. Tommy hated running, he hated hurdles, he hated long jump, he hated the whole lot. He hated the way Jason made fun of him because he was so thin, and he hated the way Gordon was so brilliant at absolutely every event.

Every Friday, it was the same thing. Straight after lunch they would line up and walk together towards the athletics field. The walk was OK. Tommy didn't mind the walk, it gave him a chance to think and to dream… Now he was Tommy Thomas, Jedi Knight, again. He wasn't walking in line with everyone else now, he was leading his own team of Jedi Knights and he was the leader, his light sabre at his side ready to be drawn at the slightest sign of trouble. He held his head high; he marched with his battalion following.

Then in the distance he saw Princess Anna. She had strayed out past Darth Mr Harris and there was a death destroyer heading straight towards her. The death destroyer let out a mighty sound…

Wait… "This isn't a dream!" Suddenly Tommy was staring at a huge lorry running down the hill and Anna really had strayed out into the road in front of it. She was going to die. Tommy looked across at Gordon. He was just staring in horror, but he wasn't moving, Mr Harris was shouting, Jason wasn't laughing now, and Anna just stood there, too afraid to move. She seemed tiny in the shadow of this huge lorry. Then Tommy ran. It was almost an instinct; maybe in his head he was still Tommy Thomas, Jedi Knight rushing to rescue the princess. Tommy didn't know why, he didn't think about it, he just ran as fast as he could towards Anna. He dived and pushed Anna out of the way.

Anna rolled out of the path of the lorry, and found herself on the pavement dazed and just a little bruised.

Tommy looked up; he looked up to the sight of an enormous lorry rushing towards him, three metres, two metres, the driver slammed on the brakes but there was no way the lorry would stop in time.

The brakes screeched.

The whole class stared at the scene as Tommy curled himself up into the tiniest ball you've ever seen. The lorry rolled over the top of him without even touching him, and when the lorry had passed, Tommy was totally unharmed. He stood up and the whole class went wild. Tommy was a hero. He had saved Anna.

The fuss lasted some weeks, the papers printed stories and took lots of pictures, then everything went back to normal. Tommy was still quite ordinary in real life, but in his dreams he was Tommy Thomas, Jedi Knight.

Tommy was average at absolutely everything, except for one thing – computers. When it came to computers, Tommy was incredible. He was so good that Mr Harris decided that Tommy should be the one to show Gordon how to use the computer. Gordon was the class leader, but he was absolutely useless with computers. Every time he tried to use the computer, things went wrong. The screen went blank; the computer crashed. It was not a pretty sight. So Tommy was to teach him.

Tommy was excited about the opportunity. In his mind, Tommy became Tommy Thomas, Jedi Knight, and Gordon became his disciple. Tommy Thomas, Jedi Knight would teach Gordon the secrets of defeating the Dark Lords. He would show him the secrets of Jedi mind control. In reality, he would just show him how to start the computer up, and how to use it. It was fairly basic, really. But Gordon didn't think of it as exciting at all. He found the whole thing very embarrassing. Tommy may have been a hero, he may have saved Anna a few weeks ago, but Gordon didn't see him as anything other than a geek who was totally obsessed with *Star Wars*.

Tommy tried to show Gordon how to start up the computer. Gordon was far too busy trying to look cool. He didn't want people to see him with Tommy. He wanted to look cool all the time. When Tommy tried to show him how to use the software, Gordon just walked up and down the classroom trying to impress the girls.

Several weeks went past, and then it was time for the end of term test. Tommy got his usual A in computers, but Gordon got an F. He didn't know how to start up the machine; he didn't even know what software was. Mr Harris called Tommy and Gordon into his office when everyone had gone home, to find out what had gone wrong. Tommy explained that he really had tried his best to teach Gordon. Gordon had to admit that Tommy had tried really hard. Gordon just hadn't tried to learn. He was too worried about what other people thought to be a proper Jedi disciple.

It was that time of year again. It was time to choose the school president. Tommy hated the way that the people who were nominated spent the week trying to get as many people as possible to vote for them. But this year it would be very different. Everyone knew that Gordon would win. Gordon was the most popular person in the whole school. All the girls liked Gordon. And all the boys looked up to him. He was the best football player, best rugby player, best at everything. Gordon was sure to win.

Everyone was so sure that Gordon would win that no one else bothered putting their name forward. But Mr Harris wasn't happy. He liked it when lots of different people were nominated to be school president. He liked the way that they tried hard to get chosen – he called this "campaigning". And he liked the fact that everyone got to vote – he called this "democracy". He was very unhappy with the fact that no one else was standing for school president. And right now Mr Harris was letting everyone in assembly know exactly how unhappy he was.

"Come on! There must be someone out there who's going to be brave enough to stand against Gordon. There must be one. We only need one person to stand up and we can do this properly," Mr Harris bellowed.

Nothing would have happened; everything would have gone smoothly, except that Tommy Thomas was dreaming again. Tommy Thomas, Jedi Knight had just rescued Princess Anna from Darth Mr Harris yet again. And now he was fighting his way past the robots. He had just reached the final stage and had to jump out of one spaceship into another. But he got so carried away with his dream that he really did jump up. There, in front of hundreds of other children, Tommy Thomas was standing.

Mr Harris just stared. There were some sniggers and there was some laughter. Then Mr Harris started to clap his hands, slowly.

"Well, well! Tommy Thomas, you really are a surprising person. It'll be great to have you in the contest. So there it is, everyone. In one week's time we will have to decide who will be the school president – Gordon or Tommy."

Tommy really didn't know what he had done until Anna explained it to him. When he realized what had happened, he was horrified. It was going to be very embarrassing. Gordon would get all the votes and he would get none, and then everyone would laugh at him – even Anna.

Monday morning came and the "campaigning", as Mr Harris called it, began. Gordon was all set. He'd had badges made, saying:

VOTE
GORDON

He was sticking them everywhere. He was walking all around the school trying to look cool, waving to people and smiling a lot. The vote would be on Friday. Tommy didn't do anything. He didn't think he had any chance, so he was just himself. And so the week progressed:

Monday:

- Gordon gave out hundreds and hundreds of his badges.

- Tommy helped Suzy to the school nurse after she cut her leg. After all, she was only seven.

Tuesday:

- Gordon put up loads of posters with his name on.

- Tommy did nothing at all except get totally confused during history – Anna had to help him and Tommy was incredibly grateful.

Wednesday:

- Gordon gave out free chocolate bars to everyone who said they would vote for him.

- Tommy bought dinner for one of the younger children after a bully tripped him up and made him drop his lunch.

Thursday:

- Gordon arrived in school wearing a T-shirt saying "Gordon for School President".

- Tommy helped some of the nine-year-olds with their computer homework. He'd totally given up on winning the contest. He never thought he had a chance anyway.

Friday:

- Gordon arrived early, wearing a T-shirt saying "THE WINNER".

- Tommy came late, he'd been dreaming on the way.

Throughout the morning, everyone had the chance to go to the dining room and vote for the person they wanted as school president. Tommy went and voted as well. He was so sure that Gordon would win that he voted for Gordon himself. Tommy just waited patiently for the voting to finish and for the result to be announced.

He was a bit surprised when Anna came up to him during the morning and smiled at him and whispered: "I voted for you, Tommy! I hate big-heads like Gordon."

He was even more surprised when a ten-year-old came to him and said: "Me and my mates have voted for you, Tommy. Thanks for helping my sister when she fell over on Monday."

And so it went on. At break-time, the guy who Tommy had bought dinner for came up to him and said: "I'm voting for you, mate! And so is my whole class. I told them what you did for me and they think it was a cool thing to do."

During lunch – Tommy spent most of his lunchtimes in the computer room – he received lots and lots of emails telling him that he would get their vote.

And sure enough, at the end of the day when the votes were counted, the result was amazing:

Gordon   **2 Votes**
Tommy   **400 Votes**

Tommy couldn't believe it. Gordon couldn't believe it either. Tommy was the new school president.

Syd Snake

Syd lived in a big forest with lots of other animals. But they tended not to mix too often because Syd was being very naughty. Syd didn't mean to be naughty. He just sort of was.

Syd liked eggs; he liked eggs very, very much. He would do anything to get eggs. The only problem was, Syd liked his eggs warm, and the only way to get warm eggs was to steal them from under the hens.

Well, on this particular day, Syd was hungry. He really wanted an egg. He slithered over to Farmer Bill's farmyard and looked around. Henrietta Hen was just laying an egg. He waited until the egg had been laid and then, slithering over, he stole it. He swallowed it in one great gulp and slithered away.

He slithered all the way to the farmyard gate and slithered underneath. Unfortunately the egg got stuck, trapping Syd. Syd pulled very hard once. Syd pulled very hard twice, until eventually the egg broke and the warm runny yoke ran down Syd's tummy. It was delicious.

The only problem is, when you start to do things wrong, it's very hard to stop.

Syd Snake

So the very next morning, Syd wanted another egg. He slithered over to Farmer Bill's farmyard and waited until Henrietta laid another egg. The same thing happened. He swallowed it, slithered back to the gate, got stuck, pulled until the egg broke and then, with a great big smile on his face, he slithered on home.

Farmer Bill was a bit concerned. Every morning he went to Henrietta, his best hen, to get an egg for breakfast, and every morning there wasn't an egg. He asked Henrietta where the eggs had gone but she just clucked and he didn't understand.

Syd couldn't stop now. Like us, once we start to do wrong things we keep on doing them. Syd kept on slithering over to the farmyard and stealing the eggs and breaking them under the gate and slithering off home, until one very sad day...

Because Farmer Bill couldn't work out where his eggs were going, he set a trap. He took an egg from another hen, hard-boiled it, and then placed it under Henrietta. Then he waited.

Eventually, Syd showed up. He slithered over like always and stole the egg. He couldn't wait to get to the gate to break the egg in his tummy. He rushed towards the gate and – nothing broke. He pulled and pulled and pulled – nothing. He was stuck.

Farmer Bill crept up behind him with his axe, and bang! He chopped Syd in two. The egg fell out.

All because Syd started doing bad things. He stole something small – just one egg – but once we start to do bad things, it's very hard to stop!

The Skaters

Once upon a time there was a magical land where the oddest creatures you have ever seen lived. They were called the Skaters. They had crash helmets in various colours on their round heads, they had thin bodies and long dangly legs, and pads the same colour as their crash helmets on their arms and legs. Now, all that may make for a strange description, but the weirdest part of all was that instead of feet they had wheels. It meant they could travel very fast and do all sorts of marvellous tricks.

On this particular day, no one was travelling around very fast and doing any marvellous tricks. In fact, no one had been travelling around and doing all sorts of marvellous tricks for the past year. An evil man had played a trick on the Skaters and had taken all their cans of oil away. This meant that when it rained, their wheels had begun to rust. And now the wheels had rusted so much that the Skaters couldn't move at all. Then, to upset the Skaters even more, the man – whose name was Evan – had placed the cans of oil just metres away from the Skaters. This meant that the Skaters could see the oil they needed, but could never actually reach it.

The Skaters

People didn't come to the Skaters's land very often, and those that did were usually friends of Evan and did nothing to help the Skaters. They were unable to move and extremely miserable for a whole year. They would probably still be there now if a friendly man named Billy Bearing had not turned up. Billy was very unusual; he wore tartan trousers, had bright red hair and spoke with a strong Scottish accent. But the most amazing thing about Billy was the huge smile he wore on his face. His entire face seemed to shine. Billy was happy on the inside and this joy shone out. Billy was a Christian; you don't get this sort of joy otherwise.

Billy took one look at the Skaters and knew what to do. He reached for a can of oil and began squirting.

"Och, a wee bit of oil here and a wee bit there," he said, "and they'll be as good as new."

Before long, all the Skaters were moving very fast and doing marvellous tricks again. They were so happy they just couldn't stop themselves. Billy became an instant hero and was presented with his very own skateboard. But after several goes and always falling on his bottom he soon decided: "Och, this skating lark is no for me. I'll stick to walking, if you don't mind."

The Skaters were overjoyed at being able to skate again and it wasn't long before their cries of fun reached the unpleasant-looking castle on the hill where Evan lived. He looked out of his window and saw the Skaters going very fast and doing marvellous tricks, and he was furious. He grabbed his bag of special stones that one of his evil friends had found for him, and set off to sort out whoever had released the Skaters from his nastiness.

Evan walked into the middle of the Skaters's town and shouted: "Who did this? Who oiled you? Who did it?"

The Skaters slammed on their brakes and looked at Evan. Some began to shake, others began to cry – but soon stopped for fear of rusting their wheels again – others looked at the ground and tried not to look into Evan's piercing eyes. The Skaters knew how evil and nasty Evan could be.

"Who did this?" Evan demanded.

"Och, I think you'll be looking for me, mister. Nice to meet you. I'm Billy Bearing."

Evan spun round and turned his piercing eyes on Billy. He expected Billy to be afraid, maybe even to run away, but instead, Billy reached out his hand and said: "Nice to meet you, sir!"

Evan just stared. Billy smiled and Evan was sure he was glowing with joy.

"Well, I'll teach you to meddle in my affairs," said Evan, and reached into his bag to get a special stone.

He lifted the stone, but Billy smiled and said: "Och, you don't want to be doing that sir, it will nay work."

Evan didn't listen. He grabbed the stone that would make Billy cry for a month. He threw the stone at Billy and waited. As Evan watched, tiny little flowers floated down around Billy. Evan gasped. Then he tried another. This one would make Billy feel as sad as it was possible to feel. But instead, a huge box of chocolates appeared in Billy's hand. The joy inside Billy was protecting him.

Finally, Evan went for his worst magic. This would make Billy think that all his relatives had died, that all the people he knew were ill, and his pets had all run away. This was surely going to get Billy. Just for good measure, Evan grabbed another stone as well. This one would turn Billy into a wobbling jelly.

Evan threw the stones. There was a huge explosion and there stood a big red jelly where Billy had been. Evan began to dance and shout and celebrate. The Skaters began to cry, even though their wheels would rust. Evan was delighted.

But then, the jelly began to change shape. Something was happening. Billy's joy wasn't just on the outside. It was all through him; he was full of joy. The jelly exploded and there stood Billy. He began to laugh. Evan hated laughter. Especially when it came from joy inside.

Evan turned and ran. He knew he was no match for real joy.

Olle and the Troll

Olle had never seen a troll. He was only five years old.

"Trolls are ugly!" said his mother. "They have noses like turnips and eyebrows like blackberry bushes."

"They are scary!" said his father. "Their mouths are like caves with huge gleaming teeth."

"Trolls are dangerous!" said his parents together. "The troll from Troll Mountain put our best goat into a sack and took it away to the mountain. You must be careful of trolls, or one will come and put you into a black bag and take you to the mountain as well."

Olle had never seen a troll, but if he did, he knew exactly what he was going to do. He was going to take his sword that he had made by nailing two pieces of wood together, and he was going to cut the nasty thing to pieces.

"I'll chop him to bits," boasted Olle. "No trolls had better show their faces around here."

"You'll do no such thing," commanded his father. "If you see a troll, you are to call for help and keep the front door locked."

Olle had never seen a troll. He was only five years old.

Olle had never seen a troll, but the troll who lived on the great mountain had seen him and had decided one day to stuff him in his sack and take him back to the mountain. So he waited for Olle's parents to start their day's work, then he tramped down the big mountain to Olle's house.

The troll disguised himself. He pulled a hood over his head, picked up a stick and pretended to limp. When he arrived at Olle's front door, he put on a croaky voice and knocked.

"Hello, I'm a stranger round here," he said, "and I'm lost. Can you come and help me?"

Olle looked out of the window. Olle had never seen a troll. He was only five years old. But if he did see a troll, he was sure that they wouldn't look like this. This was an old man with a limp.

Olle shouted, "I can't open the door. The troll from the mountain may put me into a sack and take me back to Troll Mountain if I open the door. He's already taken our best goat."

"Maybe I can help," replied the disguised troll. "I've seen a goat on the mountain. I could take you there."

"But that's where the troll lives," replied Olle. "Not that I'm scared. I've got my sword."

"Well, come on, then," said the troll.

Olle was convinced. He came out of the door and followed the disguised troll up the mountain. Olle had never seen a troll, even though he was walking up the mountain with one. He was only five years old.

Olle had brought some bread with him. He decided to stop and eat some. He offered the troll some, but everyone knows – everyone except Olle – that if a troll accepts food from you, he can't harm you. The troll refused. He was looking forward to eating Olle. Olle continued to offer the bread to the troll. He really was a very kind and loving five year old.

The troll smiled. "What if I wasn't a nice old man, but I was really a troll?"

Olle smiled back. "Don't be silly. You're a kind old man who's helping me to find my goat."

The troll was so impressed with himself and his disguise that he began to laugh out loud. Soon he would be ready to eat Olle. But Olle, seeing the troll's mouth open wide in laughter, thought it would be a great opportunity to share his lunch with him, and tossed some bread into his mouth. The troll coughed and spluttered, but eventually swallowed the bread. And everyone knows – everyone except Olle – that if a troll accepts food from you, he can't harm you.

The troll was really upset. But what could he do? He knew the rules. He was so sad that he took Olle to the goat and helped him take the goat home. Olle's parents were so pleased to see Olle again – and their best goat too – that they threw a great party.

And they wanted to invite the old man to come. But guess what? He was never seen again.

Billy the Goat

Billy the Goat lived just below the very top of the mountain, just before the snow-capped peaks. He was an angry sort of goat. Always rushing about. Always headbutting things. Always knocking things over. If he wasn't chewing grass, he was charging at rocks.

He was always quite angry, but there were days when Billy was particularly angry. Those were the days when the boys from the village would climb to the top of the mountain to tease him and call him names. Sometimes they would steal his food and run away. This made him really angry. But whenever he saw them and chased after them, they would run away down the mountain and race through the gate halfway down and close it before Billy reached it. Billy would charge at the gate as hard as he could. He would push and push at the gate, ramming and charging and butting, but the gate wouldn't open. The boys would stand the other side and laugh and giggle and make fun of Billy's goatee beard.

Billy would eventually give up, and storm off back to the top of the mountain in a major huff. He would be angrier than ever. Then he would pass Squirrel. Squirrel would make him even angrier when he would say, "I know how you could get through the gate. It's really quite easy."

But Billy wouldn't listen. He would grunt, "If I can't get through, you have absolutely no chance. Now go and eat some nuts or something."

He'd make his way back to the very top of the mountain and practise ramming some rocks. He imagined he was charging at those boys. But he knew that he'd never get the chance while that gate stayed shut.

The boys usually came every Saturday, but now that the summer holidays had arrived, they were coming every single day. Billy was angrier than ever. Every single day they would come and tease him, every single day he would charge down the mountain, every single day he would get stopped by the gate, and every single day the boys would laugh and call him names. And as if that wasn't enough, every single day Squirrel would say, "You can get past the gate, you know."

Billy hated school holiday time. The boys had been teasing him every single day for a whole month. He hated what was happening but he refused to listen to Squirrel.

Eventually, after another week had passed, Billy snapped at Squirrel, "So how do I get past the gate?"

Squirrel smiled. "Interested now, are you?"

Billy demanded: "Tell me, if you know. Tell me now!"

Squirrel remained calm. "I think you are missing a word."

Billy thought and then said, "OK! Please tell me. Please!"

Squirrel nodded, and spoke quietly. "The gate opens toward you. You need to pull and not push."

Billy couldn't believe it. It was so simple. Why hadn't he seen it?

Billy couldn't wait for the next day. The boys came up as usual, they teased him as usual, and they ran back down the mountain as usual. But today, they were surprised to see that Billy didn't charge the gate after they had gone through. They stopped and stared. Their mouths dropped open as Billy calmly used his strong horns to pull the gate open.

The boys ran as quickly as they could, but they weren't quick enough. Billy's horns rammed into them again and again. When they eventually got home they were covered in bruises and decided never to go up the mountain to tease Billy again.

Billy walked back up the mountain, triumphant. He held his head high and strutted forward. When he passed Squirrel, he stopped. He turned slowly and said, "Thank you."

Then he continued his journey to the top of the mountain.

John Jones
Gets Accused

John and Jack Jones were twins. Both were ten years old. Both were full of fun and mischief. They were always very excited and happy. But Jack was a bit naughtier than John. Jack was usually in trouble for not making his bed, or for bringing mud indoors, or for not doing his chores. John was neat, tidy, and always did his chores.

At school, Jack would spend much time in the head teacher's office being told off. John was very conscientious and never did anything to be told off for. Although John behaved well in school, he was well liked. He was the captain of the school football team and had the highest goal scoring record in the history of the school. The teachers liked John and the other children liked him too. Except for Julian Rogers. He was sure that he should have been captain of the football team. He was much faster than John and much tougher, even if he wasn't as skilful. He didn't like John at all. He tried to pick fights with him all the time, but John would just walk away shaking his head. He thought Julian was sad and not worth the effort. Jack wanted to fight Julian, but John wouldn't let him.

Jack was always in trouble for talking in class, or playing silly tricks on teachers, or writing comments on the whiteboard such as "Mr Thomas loves Mrs Andrews" which got him into lots of trouble, especially because it was the week the school inspectors were in the school. But he wasn't bad. Julian was bad. He would steal other people's things. He would get into fights and he would deliberately damage school property.

One day Julian saw his opportunity to get at John. Mrs Andrews had left her purse on the desk and Julian was the first to arrive in the classroom. He saw the purse and grabbed it. He took all the credit cards out, and then hid the purse under some books in John's desk.

The rest of the class came in and started to prepare for the lesson. They pulled their books out and Mrs Andrews was about to start teaching when she realized that her purse was missing. She gave a shriek and then stared at the class.

"Who's taken my purse?" she asked. "Nobody leaves this room until it's found. Now open your desks."

She went straight to Julian's desk first because she knew what he was like, but it was clear. She searched all the rest of the desks until she came to John's. She couldn't believe it. She never expected to find it there.

"Everyone else, go. John, stay."

Mrs Andrews called the police and John seemed to be in all sorts of trouble. Julian was so pleased with himself that he took the credit cards and went to the city to spend some money.

John was asked all sorts of questions. But the interesting thing was this: because John had never done anything wrong, Mrs Andrews didn't really think it could be John. The head teacher didn't think it could really have been John, and when the police came it didn't take them long to realize that the credit cards were missing. The answer was obvious. Whoever had the credit cards was the real thief, and after the police received a call from the music shop in the city it didn't take long to find Julian with the credit cards. He was in serious trouble.

But the great thing is this. Because John had never done anything wrong, even when people said bad things about him, they could never stick.

Pryderi the Wise

There was once a kingdom that was green and lush. The king of this land was fair and just and always did the right thing. He had three sons and a daughter. Although his wife had died many years earlier, his sons and daughter brought him great joy.

One day, disaster fell on the kingdom, when a dragon made his home there. He terrorized the people of the land and burned down many of their houses. He demanded that each family bring him a gift, starting from the beginning of the new year. The gift was to be their youngest daughter. The sacrifices would begin in three months' time, and the king's daughter, Branwen, was to be the first.

Many of the king's bravest knights tried to battle with the dragon but all were killed. The king didn't know what to do, so he summoned his wisest men and asked them how he was to rid the kingdom of the dragon. The wise men consulted their old, old books until they found recorded there the words of an ancient legend. The legend talked about the son of a king going to a faraway castle and finding out the name of the dragon. Then whoever called the dragon by its name would kill it.

The king's three sons were eager to go on the quest to the castle. Gwydion, the eldest, said, "Father, I will go, for I am the greatest warrior in the kingdom."

Callum, the second eldest, said, "Father, I will go, for I am the greatest hunter in the kingdom."

Pryderi, the youngest, said, "Father, I will go..."

But before he could say any more, his brothers started laughing. "What will you do?" they jested. "Tell the lord of the castle one of your poems?"And they laughed so much tears flowed down their cheeks.

Gwydion, the eldest, set off on his quest. He travelled for some time over mountains, through rivers, into valleys, around great forests, until eventually he arrived at the castle spoken of by the legend.

Gwydion knocked hard on the castle doors and the doors slowly opened. There stood an old lady.

"Stand aside, woman," demanded Gwydion. "I am on an important quest."

The woman did as she was ordered. Gwydion walked into the castle. Swirling mists engulfed him, weird shapes filled the air, and strange noises bombarded his senses. He looked straight ahead, and there in front of him was a golden king sitting upon a stone throne.

"Who dares approach me?" came the booming voice of the king. Gwydion began to say: "It is I, Gwydion..."

But before the sentence was completed, the king looked at the prince, a strange light came from the king's eyes, and Gwydion was turned to stone.

Many weeks went by, and then Callum, the next eldest, went to his father to ask permission to attempt the journey. After some preparation, he set off.

He travelled for some time over mountains, through rivers, into valleys, around great forests, until eventually he arrived at the castle spoken of by the legend.

Callum knocked hard on the castle doors and the doors slowly opened. There stood an old lady.

"Stand aside, woman," demanded Callum. "I am on an important quest."

The woman did as she was ordered. Callum walked into the castle. Swirling mists engulfed him, weird shapes filled the air, and strange noises bombarded his senses. He looked straight ahead, and there in front of him was a golden king sitting upon a stone throne.

"Who dares approach me?" came the booming voice of the king. Callum began to say, "It is I, Callum…"

But before the sentence was completed, the king looked at the prince, a strange light came from the king's eyes, and Callum was turned to stone.

Many weeks went by, and then Pryderi went to his father to ask permission to attempt the journey. His father wouldn't listen to him, "Your brothers are both lost, your sister is to be sacrificed to the dragon, and if I lose you as well I will surely die of a broken heart."

Pryderi loved his father very much, but he wanted to bring his brothers back and save his kingdom.

He travelled for some time over mountains, through rivers, into valleys, around great forests, until eventually he arrived at the castle spoken of by the legend.

Pryderi knocked hard on the castle doors and the doors slowly opened. There stood an old lady.

"Hello, my name is Pryderi."

After meeting his brothers, the lady was shocked to hear Pryderi being so polite.

Pryderi was a prince just like his brothers. He too could have commanded the lady to do what he wanted. He was strong like the others, but he was also gentle. He knew how to control his power. She was even more surprised when Pryderi continued, "Is there any way you can help me with my quest?"

The woman had never been treated so kindly and courteously. She explained to Pryderi that anyone who looked directly on the face of the king would be turned to stone. She gave him a special mirror.

"Approach him backwards," she instructed. "Then make your request when he asks."

Pryderi walked into the castle armed with the mirror. Swirling mists engulfed him, weird shapes filled the air, and strange noises bombarded his senses. He was walking in backwards, so he looked into the mirror and saw a golden king sitting upon a stone throne.

"Who dares approach me?" came the booming voice of the king.

Pryderi began: "It is I, Pryderi."

But never did he directly face the king; he kept looking in the mirror. "Ah!" said the king. "I see that you are a wise young man. What is your request?" Still without making eye contact, Pryderi made his request.

"I have two requests, O King. I would like to know the name of the dragon who is destroying my kingdom, and I would also like you to release my brothers." For Pryderi had seen the two stone statues of his brothers.

"I will grant your requests," replied the king. "Your brothers are fortunate that at least one of the family knows how to be kind and courteous. As for the name of the dragon, it is Browg, an old and particularly bad-tempered dragon."

The king clicked his fingers and Pryderi's brothers were released and turned back to flesh and blood.

The brothers rode home together. On arriving in the kingdom, Pryderi rode straight for the dragon. The dragon laughed as he saw Pryderi approach.

"Who are you? Such a young man to die," scoffed the dragon.

Pryderi focused his eyes on the dragon: "It is not I who will die today, it is a dragon whose name is Browg."

Horror filled the dragon's face. His name had been spoken. He exploded right in front of Pryderi. The rule of the dragon had been broken. The kingdom would recover. And one day Pryderi would be its wisest and noblest king ever.

Polly and the Frog

Polly had a very wicked stepmother. Her own mother had died when she was very small and the woman her father had married didn't like Polly. So she made Polly do the hardest jobs around the house, and if she didn't do the jobs well she was punished. As for Polly's father, he loved the woman so much that he wouldn't do anything to stop her.

One day the wicked stepmother called for Polly and very sternly said: "Girl, go to the well and fill this sieve with water. When it is full, bring it back to me."

Polly knew this was impossible. The sieve was full of holes. She couldn't do it, no one could. She walked to the well. But when she got to the well all she could do was sit down and cry.

"You don't look very happy young lady, what's the matter?"

To her amazement, Polly turned around to see the fattest, slimiest, friendliest frog she had ever seen. She was so surprised to see a talking frog that she answered almost immediately, forgetting she wasn't supposed to talk to strangers.

"It's my stepmother," she began. "She wants me to fill the sieve with water. It's impossible, I know, but if I don't do it, she'll punish me as soon as I get home."

"It's not impossible at all," the frog croaked. "I'll tell you how to do it if you promise me one thing. You must do anything I ask of you for one whole night."

"All right," Polly agreed. "Now tell me what must I do."

"Take some leaves and moss and jam them into the holes," commanded the frog, "and then fill the sieve."

Polly did what the frog suggested. It worked.

"Thank you," said Polly.

"That's OK," replied the frog. "But don't forget your promise."

Polly hurried home, and her stepmother was so amazed she didn't even find anything wrong with Polly's work. But that night, during dinner, there came a knock at the door.

"Polly, there's a frog here for you," called Polly's father from the front door.

Polly swallowed hard and walked to the front door.

"Do you mind if I come in?" asked the frog.

Well, Polly did mind very much, but she also remembered her promise and she knew how important it was to be faithful and to keep promises.

"We're just having dinner," Polly began.

"That's nice," croaked the frog. "I feel a bit hungry myself."

Polly returned to the dining room with the frog behind her. At first her stepmother looked angry, then a smile spread across her face. She thought this might be a golden opportunity to make fun of Polly.

"Oh, I see you found a new friend," sneered Polly's stepmother. "He seems a perfect match for you."

"It's hard to see anything down here," said the frog to Polly. "Can I sit on your lap?"

Polly was very unhappy, but she knew how important it was to be faithful, she knew how important it was to keep her promises. So she allowed the frog to sit on her lap. He was very slimy.

"Now, how about a bite to eat?" enquired the frog.

The stepmother was howling, she was laughing so much.

"Let's see you feed him, Polly," cackled the stepmother.

Polly scooped up a bit of her dinner and fed it to the frog.

"Perhaps the little froggy would like a drink as well?" mocked the stepmother.

"No, thank you," replied the frog, "but I do have one more request. I wonder if Polly would kiss me, right here on my cheek?"

The stepmother laughed so much she nearly fell off her chair.

"Go on, Polly, kiss your froggy friend," she said.

Polly was embarrassed.

"I thought you were my friend?" she said to the frog.

"I am," said the frog. "Trust me. Friends keep their promises."

Polly was feeling ill, but she leaned forward, shut her eyes, and kissed the frog on his green, slimy cheek. But when Polly opened her eyes, the frog had gone and, as happens in many of these stories, there in his place was the most handsome young man Polly had ever seen.

"You've done it!" he shouted, jumping off her lap and dancing for joy. "You've broken the curse and now I'm free again. Will you come with me tonight to my castle and be my princess?"

Polly looked at her father and at her stepmother. Her father looked amazed, and the wicked stepmother was no longer laughing.

"Yes," she said. "I would like that very much, but what about them?"

"Well," began the prince, looking at the stepmother, "we do have some vacancies for cleaners."

"No, it's all right!" said the stepmother hurriedly. "We'll stay right here. You visit when you want."

So Polly became Princess Polly, all because she kept her promises.

Gladys Aylward
Goes to China

On an October Saturday in 1932, Gladys Aylward left Liverpool Street Station in London for the long train ride across Europe and Russia. It was the start of a great adventure.

Four years earlier she had been sitting in class with the rest of the students. She had waited a long time to come to college. It was the college for the China Inland Mission. Gladys was sure that God had told her to go to China as a missionary, and apparently this was the best place to learn.

She had been there for three months, but she wasn't doing particularly well. She wasn't very good at reading and writing, and didn't enjoy doing all the studying. But still, God had told her to go to China, so everything would be just fine. But Gladys was in for a shock. Before the end of the lesson, she was called out of the room and asked to go to see the principal.

Gladys sat uneasily in the principal's office.

"Gladys," the principal said, gently, "your grades for the first quarter are very poor. It would be a waste of time and money for you to continue."

"But," Gladys protested, "all my life I have felt that God wants me to be a missionary in China."

"Besides," the principal went on, "by the time you graduate, you will be almost thirty. That is too old to learn a hard language like Chinese."

Shoulders sagging, she rose and began to leave the office. She was so sure that God wanted her to go to China. But she wasn't clever enough. She had been kicked out of the only college that could get her into China.

Gladys refused to accept the decision as final. She knew that there were people in China who desperately needed help. But what could she do? The college had thrown her out and she had no money to get to China. She had no college, no job, no support. But Gladys was a do-er, and she was going to do something.

She took a job as a housekeeper in South Wales, but she spent all her spare time working for the Rescue Service, helping young girls who had run away from home. While she was waiting to go to China, she would not waste her time. She would spend it helping others; she would do something.

She was determined to go to China. So one day she went to the travel agent and asked about the cheapest way to China. The travel agent told her, and then told her the price. Over the next couple of years, Gladys gave money to the travel agent until eventually she had paid enough to be able to go to China. She collected her ticket and she was ready to set off. She would do something, even if nobody else did. She may not be clever enough to get through college. She may have been told that she would never be able to go to China, but she didn't believe it. People may have said no, but she was going anyway.

She had heard that Jeannie Lawson, an elderly missionary, was looking for a younger woman to continue her work. Gladys wrote to Mrs Lawson. Mrs Lawson accepted her, but first she had to get to China. So she set off from London with her ticket, her passport, her Bible, and a couple of pounds. The journey was far from easy. The first difficulty was travelling through Germany, where the officials were not happy when they asked her why she was going to China and she simply replied, "God said." They asked her many questions. They tried to stop her continuing, but there was no way this young woman was turning back. Still, the worst was yet to come.

She travelled on through Russia. The Russians were at war with China and the journey was very hazardous. At one point, at a place called Chita, the train stopped and soldiers boarded the train and commanded everyone to get off. But Gladys protested. Her ticket said Dairen, a place on the China Sea, and she would not get off until she arrived there. The journey continued. But some miles later the train was stopped again, and this time the conductor announced that the train would not go any further for several months.

Gladys had no choice but to get off the train and walk back to Chita. It was a long walk and before long night had fallen, and with it, intense cold. She stopped to rest in a tunnel. In the background she could hear the sound of wolves howling in the Russian countryside. The wolves were coming closer, but as it turned out the morning came before the wolves, and she continued back to Chita. At Chita she boarded another train. Despite a long argument with another soldier, she insisted on being taken to Dairen. The train continued, but got no further than Vladivostok.

In Vladivostok the secret police interrogated her and would certainly have locked her in prison if a stranger hadn't helped her escape to the harbour. At the harbour she tried to get a ship to Japan, but the captain refused to take her because she had no money. Stubbornly, she pleaded with him until he agreed to take her.

She travelled from Japan to Tientsin in China, and then to the city of Yangchen. Her transport was train, bus, and mule! Most of the people in Yangchen had never seen a European person before, apart from Mrs Lawson.

The Germans said NO but Gladys kept going because God said YES.

The Russians said NO but Gladys kept going because God said YES.

The wolves could not stop her because God had said YES.

The secret police tried to stop her but God had said YES.

Even the China sea tried to stand in her way, but this was a life touched by God, this was a life that Jesus had made spectacular, nothing would or could stop her.

She would do what God had told her to do. This was a spectacular woman who lived a spectacular life.

Gladys Aylward
Rescues Children

Gladys Aylward was a Christian missionary in China. One day, she saw a woman begging by the road, accompanied by a child covered with sores and looking very hungry. Gladys was certain that this woman was not the child's mother, but had stolen the child to help her get more money from begging.

Gladys offered to buy the child, who was about five years old, for nine pennies. The woman willingly agreed. Gladys was sure she could look after the girl properly, and she was also sure that the little girl who she named Ninepence would die if she didn't get help.

This was only the beginning. A year later, Ninepence came to Gladys with an abandoned boy, saying, "I will eat less, so that he can have something." So Gladys acquired a second orphan. She named him Less. And so her family began to grow.

She became a regular and welcome visitor at the palace of the Mandarin. She dressed like the people around her. Then the war came and the Japanese invaded China. They killed many people in the villages near Gladys's village, and they bombed the city of Yangcheng, killing many others.

The Mandarin gathered the survivors and told them to retreat into the mountains. He also announced that he was impressed by the life of Ai-weh-deh – his name for Gladys – and wished to become a Christian. Gladys then led over a hundred children over the mountains to escape from the soldiers, who were intent on killing them.

She could have left at any time, she could have returned to England; after all, this was not her war. But she loved Jesus and she knew he wanted her to love the children. So she would lead these children because she was a Christian who never gave in.

Some nights they found shelter with friendly hosts. Some nights they spent unprotected on the mountainsides. Twelve days later they arrived at the river, with no way to cross it. The Japanese would surely catch up and kill them all.

The children wanted to know, "Why don't we cross?"

Gladys told them, "There are no boats."

But they said, "God can do anything. Ask him to get us across."

They all knelt and prayed. Then they sang. A Chinese officer with a patrol heard the singing. He spoke to them, heard their story, then said, "I think I can get you a boat." So they crossed the river, and eventually reached safety at a place called Sian.

Gladys was exhausted. She collapsed and was diagnosed as having typhoid. But even this could not stop her. She recovered, and then started a Christian church, opened a place to look after people with leprosy, as well as continuing to look after many children.

At the end of her life Gladys wrote of herself: "My heart is full of praise that one so insignificant, uneducated, and ordinary in every way could be used to His glory for the blessing of His people in poor persecuted China."

She never gave in. She was unstoppable.

Tortoise Brings Food

The sun was hot, the earth was dry. There had been no rain for many months. There was no food. The animals were very hungry.

The lion, the king of the beasts, called his thin and tired friends together under a tall and gnarled tree.

"The legends say that this tree is a special tree and will give us all the food we need if we can just say its secret name. But there is only one person who knows that name – the old man who lives at the top of the mountain."

"Then we must go at once," said Elephant, "as quickly as we can, before we all starve to death."

"I'll go," said Tortoise, slowly.

They all stared at him. "Don't be so silly," roared Lion. "You can't go. You're too slow and we'll all starve to death. No, we must send Hare. He will be back in no time."

Hare hurried up the side of the mountain, his long ears pulled back in the wind. He leapt, he scampered, he raced, until very soon he was standing in front of the old man.

"Please," said Hare, "tell me the name of the special tree."

The old man looked, the old man listened, and then he said: "Worn-del-hay-ma."

Hare said, "Thank you." And then he hurried back down the mountain. He leapt, he scampered, he raced, all the time saying the word "Worn-del-hay-ma".

But just as he reached the bottom of the mountain he ran straight into a huge ant hill and knocked himself silly. So silly, in fact, that by the time he reached the rest of the animals, he had forgotten the special word.

"We will have to send someone else," said Lion.

"I'll go," said Tortoise, slowly.

This time they all laughed at him.

"Don't be so silly," roared Lion. "You can't go. You're too slow and we'll all starve to death. No, we must send Elephant. He will be back in no time."

Elephant hurried up the side of the mountain, his long trunk swinging back and forth. He stamped, he tramped, and he marched, until very soon he was standing in front of the old man.

"Please," said Elephant, "tell me the name of the special tree."

The old man looked, the old man listened, and then he said: "I have already given the name to Hare, but I suppose I can tell you. The name is Worn-del-hay-ma."

Elephant said, "Thank you." And then he hurried back down the mountain. He stamped, he tramped, and he marched, all the time saying the word "Worn-del-hay-ma".

But just as he reached the bottom of the mountain he ran straight into the huge ant hill and knocked himself silly. So silly, in fact, that by the time he reached the rest of the animals, he had forgotten the special word.

"This is ridiculous," said Lion. "We will have to send someone else."

"I'll go," said Tortoise, slowly.

They all sighed.

"Don't be so silly," roared Lion. "I will go myself."

Lion hurried up the side of the mountain, his mane blowing in the wind. He leapt, he charged, he pounced, until very soon he was standing in front of the old man.

"Please," said Lion, "tell me the name of the special tree."

The old man looked, the old man listened, and then he said: "I have told Hare, and I have told Elephant, but I will tell you. It is Worn-del-hay-ma."

Lion said, "Thank you." And then he hurried back down the mountain. He leapt, he charged, he pounced, all the time saying the word "Worn-del-hay-ma".

But just as he reached the bottom of the mountain, even Lion ran straight into the huge ant hill and knocked himself silly. So silly, in fact, that by the time he reached the rest of the animals, he had forgotten the special word.

"What will we do now?" chorused the animals together.

"I'll go," said Tortoise, slowly.

Nobody said a word.

Tortoise set off.

Tortoise made his way up the mountain. He never hurried, for that is not the tortoise way. He waddled up the side of the mountain. Eventually, after quite some time, he was standing in front of the old man.

"Please," said Tortoise, "tell me the name of the special tree."

The old man looked angry, but the old man listened, and then he said: "I have already told Hare and Elephant and Lion. I will tell you, but if you forget, I will not tell anyone else. The word is Worn-del-hay-ma."

Tortoise said, "Thank you. I will not forget." Then he waddled back down the mountain. He walked slowly around the huge ant hill and joined the rest of the animals. All the animals looked very anxious. Tortoise spoke slowly: "The word is Worn-del-hay-ma. It is not such a hard word really."

The tree delivered all the food they needed, and Tortoise became a hero. Tortoise had saved everyone.

Jackie Pullinger in the Walled City

The area of Hong Kong known as the Walled City where Jackie Pullinger worked was a terrible place to be. There were shops that sold everything. Next to a shop that sold secondhand furniture there was a shop that sold food, and next to the shop that sold food there was a shop that sold children. Boys and girls were sold because their parents couldn't afford to keep them any longer.

Most of the children who lived in the Walled City never finished school. They dropped out; many of them became criminals, many of them starting selling drugs, many of them began taking drugs.

Jackie knew that God cared for these people very much, but she didn't really know what to do. She decided to rent her own shop and run it as a youth club. She would have table tennis and games, and then she would tell them about God. But even though she had good ideas and really wanted to help, it didn't seem to work. Lots of young people came to the youth club and they enjoyed the games and the table tennis, but none of them seemed interested in learning about God.

For a whole year Jackie kept opening the youth club, and for a whole year lots of young people came and had fun. But none of them wanted to learn about God. This was difficult for Jackie. She knew that they desperately needed Jesus. They needed to learn about a God who loved them. Their lives were full of junk and garbage, the stuff the Bible calls sin. Without God, they would never go to heaven. Without God, they would never have all that junk taken away from their lives.

Then Jackie realized something very important. She would never be able to help these people. She would never be able to get them to heaven; she would never be able to take all their sins away. This was God's job. Only Jesus, who is God, could take away this sin. Only Jesus.

So Jackie began to pray that Jesus would do just that. That Jesus would help the young people to find out about him. Jackie prayed every morning.

Then one day as Jackie came to the youth club, she found a young man leaning against the wall outside. He had a sweatband on his head. It showed everyone that he belonged to a Triad gang called the 14K. The Triad gangs ruled the Walled City. They sold drugs and murdered people and were always fighting with other gangs. The 14K had been in a fight with another gang, called the Jin Yu, and the young man had been hurt. Jackie helped the man, whose name was Christopher. She protected him until he was better. Then she allowed Christopher to leave.

She wasn't sure that Christopher would ever return, but she kept remembering that only Jesus could help Christopher. She kept praying. Only Jesus!

Then one day, Christopher returned to the youth club. He had come to ask Jackie the question, "Jackie, why do you bother to do what you do?"

Jackie smiled and simply answered, "Because Jesus bothered."

She took Christopher to a quiet area and began to explain why only Jesus could help him. She asked Christopher if he remembered the way his T-shirt looked on the nights he got beaten up. Christopher nodded. He remembered how his T-shirt sometimes got stained with blood. Then Jackie asked him what he did with the T-shirt. Christopher remembered he took off his bloodstained T-shirt and got a clean one.

Jackie said, "Christopher, that is what Jesus wants to do with your heart. He wants to take your stained, dirty heart, your heart that is stained by the wrong things you have done and replace it with a clean heart, a pure heart."

Christopher gave his life to Jesus, and before long many others followed. Only Jesus was to able change Christopher's heart. Only Jesus was able to help all those people in the Walled City.

The Golden Box

Karen lived alone with her father. Her mother had moved to another country many years before. Karen did miss her mum, but living with Dad was OK.

Karen had spent the whole afternoon at the kitchen table with the scissors. Dad could hear lots of cutting sounds as he sat in the living room watching television.

But when Dad eventually went to the kitchen to investigate, he was furious.

"What a waste of money! Why have you used that good wrapping paper? You really are a silly girl."

Her dad told her off quite severely. They didn't have much money, and the last thing Karen's father wanted was for her to waste their most expensive wrapping paper on her game. She had cut the gold wrapping paper up and now it was no good for anything. He grew even more upset when, after sending her to her room for cutting the paper up, he saw her pasting it onto an old box.

"What are you doing that for?" he protested. "We could have used that paper for your granny's present."

A little later, the same gold-wrapped present appeared under the Christmas tree, and when Dad looked at the tag his anger soon subsided. He felt almost embarrassed when he saw his name on the tag.

That night was Christmas Eve and Karen went to bed early – as everyone does on Christmas Eve – hoping that the morning might come more quickly. Eventually, after a very sleepless night, Karen rushed into her dad's bedroom at 6 a.m. She shook him until he eventually woke up. He was still very sleepy. He rubbed his eyes until the sleepiness had all gone. Then he stumbled into the bathroom to throw cold water over his face, and made his way downstairs. He was feeling a bit grumpy about being up so early, but he smiled as Karen opened her presents. The Barbie doll and the lovely outfits, the new slippers, pyjamas with Harry Potter on them, new school shoes… eventually all her presents were opened and all that remained under the tree was the golden box.

Karen went to collect it and handed it to Dad. He decided that he didn't mind being woken up at 6 a.m. for it must be a very lovely present to be put inside such a wonderfully decorated box. He took his time opening the lid and then he gazed inside.

But he became quite angry as he looked into the box. He looked at his little girl and spoke to her very sharply. "Young lady, don't you know that when you give a present to someone there's supposed to be something inside?"

The little girl looked up with tears in her eyes and said: "Oh, Daddy, it's not empty. I blew kisses into it until it was full. And then I put the lid on so none could escape. I've made you a box full of love."

Dad said nothing, but tears ran down his cheeks as he hugged his little girl tight.

The Young King

It was the night before his coronation, the night before he would be crowned king, and the prince sat on his bed in his royal chambers. He thought through the events of recent times. It had been a strange couple of weeks, for up until very recently he had lived in the heart of the jungle with the wild animals that he loved deeply. But as the old king lay dying, he had confessed to having a secret son who had been taken to live in the jungle. There he looked after the animals. So, a search party had been sent to find him. When they found him, the king's men could not believe that this boy could ever be a king. He held a long shepherd's crook, he had a dirty face, very few clothes, and long tangled hair. He had been brought to the palace. He was washed, his hair was cut, and he was dressed in the finest clothes. And those who saw him had to admit he looked remarkably like the old king.

Even though – or possibly because – he'd grown up in the jungle, the young king loved beautiful things. On one occasion, a courtier had walked into the main hall to discover him staring at a beautiful picture. On another occasion, a doorkeeper found him admiring a newly found statue. The young prince loved all things beautiful, but tonight, the night before his coronation, he found himself enthralled by the most beautiful things he had ever seen. They were the things he would be wearing for his coronation – the ceremony where he would be crowned king: the golden robe made with real gold thread, the sceptre with rows of pearls, and the ruby-studded crown.

Outside he could see the huge dome of the cathedral, he could hear a nightingale singing in a nearby orchard, and the warm breeze drifted over his face from the open window. He lay on his bed and looked at his finely decorated ceiling. He turned to look at that exquisite outfit and slowly his eyelids came down and he was asleep.

As he slept he dreamed a dream, and this was his dream…

He found himself in an attic with a low ceiling. At various positions around the small attic were children hard at work at weaving looms, preparing something.

"What are you doing?" enquired the young king.

The old lady who was in charge of the children looked up. "Are you a spy sent by our master the king?"

The young king didn't understand. He looked around the room and saw how hungry the children looked and how fragile and pale they were. The old woman looked tired and haggard. Then he saw the thread that they worked with. He saw how golden it was and how fine; so fine that it often cut the children's fingers.

"Why are you doing this?" asked the young king.

The woman looked up and with contempt in her eyes said: "For the new king's coronation robe."

The young king woke up. The moon was high in the sky. He eventually went to sleep again and dreamed another dream. This was his dream…

He dreamed that he was on a large ship rowed by a hundred slaves who were chained to their oars. After some time, the ship stopped and the anchor was dropped. A young boy was taken and a large weight tied to his waist. He climbed down a ladder which descended to the sea far below. After some time, the boy came back up the ladder clutching a large pearl in his hand. The captain of the ship seized the pearl and sent the boy back into the water. Again and again the boy descended on the ladder into the sea, not returning until he had a pearl in his hand. This went on for some time, until eventually he climbed up the ladder with a very large pearl, but as he handed it to the captain he fell over and died. The captain laughed and threw the body over the side of the ship.

"Why have you done this?" enquired the young king.

"We have been sent to collect pearls for the sceptre of the young king," the captain replied.

The young king woke up with a start. The moon was descending. He looked at his sceptre. His mind was full of many thoughts but eventually he went back to sleep. As he slept he had a third and final dream. This was his dream…

He was in a desert and many men were digging in the sand. A man whipped them and commanded them to dig. When the sun was high in the sky and the men became very thirsty, the man kept whipping and demanding that they dig. Many of the men fell to the ground and died because of the heat but the man made them keep digging. Eventually one man pulled a single ruby from the ground and was rewarded with a drink of water.

"Why do you make these men do this?" asked the young king. "Many of them are dying."

"And many more will die before we have enough rubies for the king's crown," replied the man with the whip.

"Which king do you do this for?" asked the young king.

The man held up a mirror and said: "Look here and you will see him."

The young king looked, and seeing his own reflection, screamed and woke up. The moon had completely gone. The sun was beginning to rise, and the day of the coronation had arrived. The royal servants came in and held up the robe and the sceptre and the crown, ready for the king to wear. The king looked at them and they were very beautiful. But his dreams still echoed in his head and he commanded: "Take them away, for they are indeed beautiful, but no item is so beautiful that people should suffer and die for it."

They thought the young king had gone crazy and the prime minister was called. He tried to persuade the king to reconsider, but the king would not listen.

The king bathed himself in clean water and then put on the old tunic that he had worn in the jungle instead of the golden robe. He took his old shepherd's crook in his hand instead of the sceptre of pearls and, reaching onto the balcony, he wove a crown out of the ivy branch which grew outside. This he wore instead of the crown of rubies.

When the prime minister saw the outfit the king wore, he protested strongly, "Your Highness, the people are expecting you dressed as a king, not as a beggar."

But the young king would not listen. He made his way to the stables, and choosing a dappled horse, he began his ride through the crowded streets to the cathedral where he was to be crowned king. The people laughed and mocked his appearance, but still he rode on. He would not wear things which people had to suffer and die to make.

Eventually he arrived at the cathedral and the archbishop met him on the steps. "Your Highness, what is this? Why are you dressed in such a way?"

"Because," replied the young king, "people are more important than things."

The archbishop didn't know what to say. The young king began his walk towards the throne where he was to be crowned. The doors of the cathedral were flung open and there stood all the nobles of the kingdom in their finest clothes, with swords drawn – dukes, lords, and earls. They were ready to slay the king. They felt that he had embarrassed them and the kingdom, and for this he would die. The king saw the men approaching and he knelt to pray. And after he had prayed, he stood up and looked at the advancing men, sadly.

And then... through the painted windows came sunlight streaming upon him, and the sunbeams wove around him and made his robes appear finer than any that had ever been made. The shepherd's crook in his hand, made of wood long dead, burst into life, and flowers of white adorned it, far prettier than any pearl ever found. The crown of ivy on his head also blossomed and flowered red, far prettier than even the prettiest rubies.

There stood the king, the finest king the kingdom had ever seen. Music bellowed from the organs, the choirboys sang. The noblemen dropped their swords, and fell to their knees. The face of the archbishop became pale as he said, "One greater than I has crowned you king." And he lifted his eyes to heaven. "Surely God thinks things are far less important than people, too."

The Girl Who Wanted Blue Eyes

Amy Carmichael was born the week before Christmas in 1867 in a little Irish village on the coast of Northern Ireland. She lived in an old cottage with her mother, her father, three sisters, and four brothers.

From the time she could remember, Amy loved colours. She loved all sorts of colours, but most of all Amy loved blue. She loved the blue of the sea near her house, she loved the blue of the sky in summer, she loved her blue dress that she wore to church on Sundays, but most of all she loved the blue of her mother's eyes. Her mother had the bluest of blue eyes and Amy began to wish for blue eyes. Amy's eyes were full of mischief, often sparkling, but brown.

Every Sunday, Amy set off for church with her brothers and sisters. She had listened to the church leader talking many times, but on this particular Sunday, just before her fourth birthday, she heard some very interesting words: "God always answers prayers!" Amy lifted up her head and heard the words again: "God always answers prayers!"

That night, she made her way upstairs to bed. She cleaned her teeth. She washed her face. Having heard the words that very morning, but being only three years of age, she knelt beside her bed and prayed, "God, I would like blue eyes like my mother's, by the morning, please. Amen." She climbed into bed, pulled the blankets over her head, and fell fast asleep, confident that when she woke up in the morning she would have blue eyes.

She woke just after the sun came up, and went straight to the bathroom to look at her new blue eyes. She was too small to see in the mirror. She reached for a nearby stool and stood on it. She opened her eyes very slowly and stared in the mirror. There, staring back at her, were a pair of the brightest, sparkling, most mischievous… brown eyes.

Amy burst into tears and ran into her mother's bedroom.

"Mum, Mum! Wake up. The man in church told me a lie."

Her mother smiled. Not a cruel smile but a kind, understanding smile. Amy's mother tried to explain: "Amy, when we're about to have dinner and you ask for cookies, and I say no, is that an answer? And what about when you ask if you can go out to play and it's raining, and I say no, is that an answer?"

Amy thought quickly. "Ummm, yes."

Amy's mum explained, "God always answers, but sometimes he says no."

Amy was confused. Why did God say no? She knew that her mother sometimes said no to her when she had eaten too many sweet things and wanted more. Her mother would say, "No, if you eat any more then you'll be sick." Her mother said no because she knew what was best for her. Maybe God had said no for a reason. But what reason?

When Amy grew older, she became a missionary and travelled to India to tell people about Jesus. She found India quite difficult. She couldn't speak the language. The weather was very, very hot and sticky, and she didn't understand the strange customs they had. She tried very hard to mix with the people, but she was a white woman and she stood out. No one would talk to her.

She visited the market and nobody would serve her, she talked to people in the street but they ignored her, she went to visit people in their homes, but she wasn't invited in. But eventually she had an idea. She mixed a coffee-coloured powder with some water and began to paint the substance onto her face, until her skin was the same colour as someone from India. She was about to walk out into the street when one of her friends said: "It's good you don't have blue eyes. If you did, people would know that you weren't Indian."

And now in the marketplace they would serve her, and in the street people would talk to her, and when she visited people's homes, they invited her in.

Amy remembered her childhood prayer and smiled. "So that's why God said no."

The Three Trees

Once, a farmer went out to sow three special seeds. He prepared the ground and planted them in just the right place. He watered them and the sun shone on them. He watered them. The sun shone on them. He watered some more. The sun shone some more. And they grew and grew and grew and grew, until they had grown into three of the tallest trees in the forest.

Every day the trees would talk to each other. They would talk about the way the sun shone, they would talk about the squirrels that ran up and down their branches, they would talk about the way the wind blew. But always they would come back to the same subject. They would ask each other: "What do you want to be when you are eventually chopped down and made into something by the carpenter?"

The trees thought very hard about the question. Maybe a rocking horse, or a doll's house, maybe a great big chair. They thought long and hard until each of them had made up their minds.

"I'd like to be a bed for a king," said the first tree.

"I'd like to be a ship for a king," said the second.

"I'd like to be a signpost to show people the way to go," said the third.

And they were decided.

Many years went past. The trees talked about many other things, but always they thought about what they wanted to be. For forty years the conversations continued, until eventually the day came when the carpenter arrived to chop down the trees.

He took his axe and chopped down the first tree.

The carpenter took the tree away and began to work. He sawed and hammered, and hammered and sawed. He took out his chisel and mallet and chopped away some of the edges. He took out his sandpaper and took off the rough bits. And then it was done. There it was. It was finished.

The tree was so excited. "I'm going to be a bed for a king."

And then he looked at himself. What he saw made him miserable. Not a bed for a king but an old feeding trough for animals. How could it have gone so badly wrong?

The carpenter took him and placed him in a stable, and the tree felt very sad.

The carpenter took the second tree away and began work. He sawed and hammered, and hammered and sawed. He took out his chisel and mallet and chopped away some of the edges. He took out his sandpaper and took off the rough bits. And then it was done. There it was. It was finished.

The tree was so excited. "I'm going to be a ship for a king."

And then he looked at himself. What he saw made him miserable. Not a ship for a king but an old fishing boat.

Some fishermen came and took him away. Every day they would set out to sea. They'd fill their nets with fish and then empty them into the boat. And the tree felt very sad.

The carpenter took the third tree away and began work. He sawed and hammered, and hammered and sawed. He took out his chisel and mallet and chopped away some of the edges. He took out his sandpaper and took off the rough bits. And then it was done. There it was. It was finished.

The tree was so excited. "I'm going to be a signpost for people everywhere."

And then he looked at himself. What he saw made him miserable. Not a signpost but a lump of wood. He felt the saddest of all the trees.

And that's where they stayed. One feeding trough, one fishing boat, and one lump of wood which the carpenter eventually gave to some soldiers.

That could have been the end. Just three ordinary objects feeling a bit sad. But it's not the end. Jesus came. And Jesus is very good at taking objects that feel ordinary and sad and doing amazing things with them.

It started right at the beginning of Jesus' life on earth. God decided to send Jesus into the world. And so Jesus was born in a stable. There was no bed, so he was placed in a feeding trough for animals. Yes, you guessed it, in the feeding trough made from the first tree. The tree that wanted to be a bed for a king became a bed for the King of all kings – King Jesus himself.

When Jesus was older, so many people wanted to hear him speak that he was forced to move further and further backwards, almost into the sea. So he climbed onto a fishing boat and spoke to the people on the coast of Galilee. And so the second tree, the one that wanted to be a ship for a king became a ship for the King of all kings – King Jesus.

And when Jesus' time on this earth was nearly finished, he died on a cross – nothing more than a lump of wood. He hung there for the wrong things we had all done. And three days later, he rose from the grave. And, of course, that lump of wood was the third tree, shaped into a cross. The tree that wanted to show all people which way to go became the tree that was to show all people the way to heaven. A signpost to heaven. The cross.

The trees' ambitions were fulfilled in the strangest ways. But that's what Jesus does. He takes ordinary objects and, often not in the way we expect, he does something great. And the three trees were the happiest trees in the entire world. They became what they wanted and more. All because of King Jesus.

Hands That Help

Albrecht and Albert Dürer were brothers. They knew everything about each other – of course they would, they'd grown up together. And they cared for each other deeply.

After the death of their parents, they'd continued to live in the same house they grew up in. Both were very talented in lots of areas, but most particularly they were brilliant artists. Both of them desired nothing more than to become famous painters; painters who would be known all over the world.

They worked very hard. They wanted to be famous; to have people all over the world paying money to own one of their paintings. Each night they would kneel in prayer and thank God for his wonderful creation: the marvellous sunsets they watched in the evenings and the incredible plants, flowers, and trees that they loved to paint.

The only problem was that neither of them could fully concentrate on their painting. They were far from famous, and on the rare occasion that one of their paintings did sell it only earned them a very small amount of money – just enough to buy new paints and a new canvas to paint on. Because only a very small amount of money came in for food and clothes and for their home, both Albrecht and Albert had to have other jobs. Albrecht was a postman and worked at delivering the town's mail. He would get up very early and walk a long way carrying a very heavy bag. Albert worked for the baker. He helped with the baking and delivered the bread to the homes in the area. He too had to get up very early, but at least he got to bring some of the leftover bread home.

Because both men got up very early, they had to go to bed quite early as well. So there was very little time for them to paint. They both wanted to be famous artists, but they knew they would never make it unless they could find more time to paint.

They continued their routine as they had always done. They worked, they tried to fit in some painting, they said their prayers, and they went early to bed every day of the week, except on Sundays when they got the chance to go to church and then spend the entire afternoon painting. They liked Sundays very much. But still, there was not enough time to paint. They knew they could be famous if they just had enough time.

It was Albert who had the idea; an idea that showed just how much he really cared for Albrecht: "I know what we must do. I will find a different job that pays more money and I will work at it all day. You will then be free to stay and paint. And when you have become famous and you are being paid lots of money for your paintings, then I can give up my job and return to my painting."

Albrecht wouldn't agree.

"No! You stay at home and paint and I'll go to work."

Albert refused to listen. "It was my idea and you must stay and paint."

So that is what happened. Because Albert cared so much for Albrecht, he was prepared to put the things he wanted to do to one side and help his brother. Albert woke up very early every morning and made his way to his new job. He'd got a job at the quarry and every day he left very early, spent the day hammering, dragging out rocks, and pushing large wheelbarrows, and when he returned home it was always very late. He would be so tired that he ate his dinner, knelt beside his bed, said his prayers, and crawled into bed where he would very quickly be fast asleep.

The quarry was hard work. Albert would have to hammer pieces of rock out of the cliff face, carry those rocks to the wheelbarrow and then push the wheelbarrow to a different part of the quarry. This he did from seven in the morning until seven at night. He didn't like the job but he dragged himself out of bed every morning because he cared for his brother. Every night he knelt and thanked God for the strength to face another day.

Albrecht painted and painted. He painted sunsets and sunrises; he painted fields at harvest-time and fields in springtime. He painted people on the streets. He painted and painted until eventually he was so good that his paintings began to sell, and people began to pay a lot of money for them. But this had taken many years. Then one day one of his paintings sold for £10,000. He was rich; £10,000 was a huge amount of money in those days. Albert would never need to work again. Albrecht couldn't wait to tell him.

Albrecht waited until Albert came home that night and then showed him the money. Albert was very happy for his brother. Albrecht proclaimed, "Albert, you never need work again. I have enough money now, you too can return to your painting. And you too can become a famous artist."

Albert smiled at his brother and then lifted his hands. Albert's hands were scarred and worn. They would never be able to hold a paintbrush properly; they would never be able to paint. Albert hadn't just given up his time to help Albrecht, he had given up his dream of becoming a famous artist as well. Albert knelt beside his bed to say thank you to God for making Albrecht so famous.

Albrecht stood in front of his painting easel and, with tears in his eyes, painted the hands that had given up everything to help him. Hands that had sacrificed.

Hands That Help

The praying hands became one of Albrecht's most famous of all paintings. Hands that help others are the loveliest hands of all.

Sam is Special

(A story for younger children)

Sam was Emily's teddy bear. He had been Emily's teddy bear for as long as he could remember and he was fed up with being a teddy bear.

"I'm fed up," he said. "I don't want to be a teddy bear."

He went for a walk by the side of the canal. As Sam walked, he saw some ducklings on the water swimming after the mother duck.

"That looks like much more fun than being a teddy bear," he thought. "I'll be a duck."

Sam made his way down to the water, tucked his legs in front of him and jumped in. He floated along for a couple of seconds and then as you would expect – *Glug! Glug! Glug! Glug!* He sank to the bottom of the canal.

Luckily, who should be walking past but Emily and her mum. Mum reached in and pulled him out. Emily took him home and Mum put him in the washing machine. Round and round he went. Then Emily put the hairdryer on him and it blew until he was dry.

"Now, listen to me, Sam bear," Emily said. "You're not a duck. God didn't make you a duck. He made you a teddy bear because that's what he wanted you to be."

Sam listened and nodded. But he still felt fed up.

"I'm still fed up," he said. "I don't want to be a teddy bear."

He went for another walk by the side of the canal. As Sam walked, he looked and on the path he saw a hedgehog rolled up in a ball.

"That looks more fun than being a teddy bear," he thought. "I'll be a hedgehog."

Sam went home, got some clothes pegs and stuck them all over himself. Then he made his way to the top of the hill besides the canal, rolled himself up in a ball and tried to be a hedgehog. But he lost his balance, rolled down the hill, and SPLASH! Where do you think he ended up? Yes, in the canal.

He floated along for a couple of seconds and then – *Glug! Glug! Glug! Glug!* He sank to the bottom of the canal.

Luckily, who should be walking past but Emily and her mum. Mum reached in and pulled him out. Emily took him home and Mum put him in the washing machine. Round and round he went. Then Emily put the hairdryer on him and it blew until he was dry.

"Now, listen to me, Sam bear," Emily said. "You're not a hedgehog. God didn't make you a hedgehog, and God didn't make you a duck. He made you a teddy bear because that's what he wanted you to be."

Sam listened and nodded. But he still felt fed up.

"I'm still fed up," he said. "I don't want to be a teddy bear."

He went for another walk by the side of the canal. As Sam walked, he looked up and flying high above the canal was a bird.

"That looks more fun than being a teddy bear," he thought. "I'll be a bird."

Sam made his way to the top of the hill and then to the swing park and then to the top of the climbing frame. He jumped off and started to flap his arms with all his might. He was trying to fly. But everyone knows that teddy bears can't fly. He flapped his arms as hard as he could, but very soon he started falling. Down and down he went until eventually SPLASH! Where do you think he ended up? Yes, in the canal.

He floated along for a couple of seconds and then – *Glug! Glug! Glug! Glug!* He sank to the bottom of the canal.

"Where's Emily and her mum?" he thought. "Where's Emily?"

Emily was nowhere to be seen. So there he sat at the bottom of the canal waiting, feeling very wet and very, very sad.

Eventually Emily and her mum came walking past. Mum reached in and pulled him out. Emily took him home and Mum put him in the washing machine. Round and round he went. Then Emily put the hairdryer on him and it blew until he was dry.

"Now, listen to me, Sam bear," Emily began. "You're not a bird. God didn't make you a bird. And God didn't make you a hedgehog, and God didn't make you a duck. He made you a teddy bear because that's what he wanted you to be."

Then Emily hugged Sam. Sam liked being hugged very much. He didn't feel so fed up now. Maybe it wasn't so bad being a teddy bear after all.

God made you *you*, because he wanted you to be you.

32

The Selfish Giant

Every day after school, the children would play in the giant's garden. They played in the giant's garden in the springtime, when the garden was full of the most amazing smells as the flowers burst into bloom. They played in the giant's garden in the summer, when the sun warmed their faces and they could feel the soft grass beneath their feet. They played there in the autumn, when they would hide under giant leaves, and they played there in the winter, when they could make snowmen and throw huge snowballs.

Every day after school, the children played in the giant's garden.

Then one day, the giant returned home. He'd been away on a long journey which had lasted several years. But now he was back. He walked into the garden and could not believe what he saw. All these horrible children playing in his garden!

"Get out," he roared. "This is my garden."

The giant was as tall as a giraffe and as wide as an elephant. So the children didn't wait to be told again. They turned and ran out of the garden as fast as their legs would carry them. Then the giant nailed up a sign saying:

KEEP OUT.

And just to be extra careful, he built a big wall around the garden so that nobody would be able to sneak in again.

Every day after school, the children now had nothing to do. They would try to think up interesting games. But nothing seemed as good as the fun they used to have in the garden. So they would sit outside the wall and remember how much they enjoyed playing in the garden before the giant came back. They remembered how much fun they'd had in the summer with the soft grass, how much fun they'd had in the autumn with those giant leaves, how much fun they'd had in the winter with those huge snowballs, and how much fun they'd had in the spring with those gorgeous flowers.

It was springtime right now. Springtime everywhere except in the giant's garden. In the giant's garden it was still winter. Spring had come to the garden, but seeing how selfish the giant was, she had left straightaway. Winter, seeing that Spring wasn't going to stay, decided to live there all year round. He spread his white snowy cloak across the ground and painted all the tress in glistening frost. He invited his friend the North Wind to join him, and so the North Wind came and howled and blew around the garden. And the North Wind invited his friend Hail to come, so Hail threw giant hailstones at the giant's castle, rattling all the roof slates until cracks appeared and North Wind could move around inside the castle, making everything cold. The giant hated Winter and couldn't wait for Spring to come. But Spring never did. So the giant wrapped himself up in a warm coat and became more and more miserable every day.

One morning, the giant was lying in bed dreaming about sunshine and happier days when he thought he heard a flute playing in his garden. He listened again. No, not a flute; it was a bird singing. He jumped up and ran to the window. As he looked into the garden he couldn't believe his eyes. Spring had come. The trees had burst into blossom, the grass was the greenest green, the birds sang, and the sun shone. And there in each of the trees was a little child happily sitting and listening to the birds.

The giant didn't know what to do. "All these children are back. They came through that hole in the wall, I reckon. I knew I should have fixed it." But then he realized: "Hey, the children are back and so is Spring. Spring must have stayed away because I was so selfish. Oh, I wish I hadn't been so selfish."

And with that he rushed out into the garden to tell the children that they could play in the garden from now on. But when the children saw the giant coming they were so scared they turned and ran away as fast as they could. The giant shouted for them to come back, but this just made them run all the faster.

However, one little boy was trying so hard to reach up into the trees that he never saw the giant coming up behind him. He jumped up but couldn't reach the branches. He jumped again and again and again but he couldn't reach. And the giant came closer. The little boy jumped again. The giant stood right behind him. The little boy jumped again. The giant caught him by the waist and lifted him into the tree. And the little boy was so excited about being in the tree that he forgot to be afraid. Then he turned around and saw the giant. The little boy was so happy he jumped into the arms of the giant and gave him a hug around his neck (well, half his neck, he only had little arms and the giant had a very large neck). The giant had never been hugged before and he liked it.

When the other children saw that the giant had become so nice, they all rushed back into the garden. The giant knocked down the wall and the children played freely in the garden from that time on. The giant even played with them, he played blind man's buff – being very careful not to stand on anybody, of course. And he tried to play skipping – but he kept causing earthquakes so he had to stop that. Then he tried football – but he kept kicking the ball so hard it would land in the next town, so the children said he couldn't play that any more.

The giant liked playing with the children, but every day the giant would ask the same question: "Have you seen the little boy that I lifted into the tree?" And every day he got the same answer: "No. We'd never seen him before and we've never seen him since."

The giant grew older and older. The children who'd crept through the hole in the wall had now grown up and their children were playing in the garden. But every day the giant still asked: "Have you seen the little boy that I lifted into the tree?" But they hadn't seen him. They didn't even know who the giant was talking about.

One winter morning, the giant was lying in his bed having a little sleep when he heard that flute sound again. No, not a flute; it was a bird singing. "That's strange," he thought. "Spring shouldn't be here for months yet."

He got up and looked out of the window. There was the little boy underneath a tree. The giant couldn't believe it. He grabbed his walking stick, and without taking off his pyjamas, he ran towards the little boy as fast as he could. He didn't even think about how strange it was that the little boy hadn't changed at all. The giant was so excited. He was smiling and incredibly happy. He had so missed this little boy. But when he finally arrived, his joy turned into anger, his joy into fury, for the little boy had scars on his hands and on his feet.

"Who did this?" he shouted. "Tell me and I'll hurt them!"

The little boy smiled and said: "It's OK, Giant. I've forgiven them for what they did." And then the boy continued: "Many years ago, you let me play in your garden and I really did enjoy it. Today, I've come to take you to my garden in heaven where you can play for ever."

The giant was just a little bit scared when he realized for the first time who this little boy was. But he took the little boy's hand and the little boy led the giant into his garden in heaven.

That day, when the children came to play in the giant's garden, they found the giant dead underneath the most beautiful tree.

The Selfish Giant

Although it was winter, the tree had burst into blossom, and the blossom had fallen, covering the giant's body in the most beautiful colour. But of course, this was just the giant's body. The giant himself was no longer there; he had gone to play in the garden of the little boy.

The Boxer

Mark was thirteen when he went to the boxing gym for the very first time. He'd been a boxing fan for a long time and something made him sure he'd be a great boxer. He had his new shorts and vest, and the man who owned the place let him borrow some gloves. Mark danced around punching bags, skipping, and thinking he was the best. He got one of the punchbags and was punching this bag as hard as he could. It wasn't moving much, but he kept punching and punching because he was sure he was a natural.

At the end of the evening, he thought he was the best boxer in the entire world and walked along with his arms stretched out wide as if he was a bodybuilder with the biggest muscles. But because he was walking along with his arms out wide and his head in the air he didn't see the other boy walking past, and he knocked into him.

The other boy looked at Mark and said, "Hey, mate, watch where you're going." He said it very politely, but Mark was having none of it.

He looked at him and with his toughest voice said, "Listen here, mate, you don't tell me to watch where I'm going because I'm tough and if you mess with me I'll knock you out."

The Boxer

The boy was much smaller than Mark. He had ginger hair, and he was wearing an old tracksuit and his trainers had holes in them. Mark was absolutely sure he could fight him. But the boy was very relaxed. He looked up at Mark and said, "Do you really want to fight me?"

Mark was a bit shocked, but he couldn't back down. Anyway, Mark was much taller and he had new shorts and a new vest and new trainers. He could take him. "Yes. I want to fight you," he said.

To Mark's surprise, the boy didn't want to fight just then. He wanted Mark to come back the following week and fight in the boxing ring.

Mark took that week very seriously. He ate lots of cereal. He went jogging every day. He did lots of press-ups and sit-ups and was sure he was going to win. He asked his friends (all four of them) to come along and the following week he got into the ring early to do some warm-ups before the other boy arrived. Mark was dancing around inside the ring and his friends were all calling his name. He was sure he was going to win. There was no doubt in his mind.

Then the gym doors opened and the other boy – whose name was Tony – walked in with about thirty friends all shouting his name and getting very excited. Mark was shocked but didn't worry. He was still much bigger. Tony got into the ring and took off his old tracksuit top – he was huge, he had muscles everywhere. The referee came and Mark and Tony walked into the middle of the ring. Mark looked down at him and said, "I'm going to take you down."

Tony just laughed.

The bell went and out came Mark, dancing and doing all sorts of funny steps. Tony walked out slowly. He was very relaxed. Mark was dancing around for about ten seconds. Then Tony's hand moved so fast nobody could see it, least of all Mark. It connected with Mark's nose, the fight was over, and Mark was flat on the floor.

That was the last thing Mark remembered before they revived him in the changing rooms. Tony had knocked him out cold. The man who owned the club looked down at Mark and smiled. "You do know who Tony is, don't you?" he asked.

"Of course I do," Mark replied. "He's the little guy with the old tracksuit and holes in his trainers."

The owner laughed. "That's true, but do you know that he's also the Welsh under sixteens boxing champion?"

Mark felt foolish. Some lessons are definitely learnt the hard way.

The Signalman's Son

David Evans was a very happy man. For him, life revolved around two things; his work and his son, and he loved both dearly.

David worked in a signal box near where the railway line crossed over a long bridge. His job was quite easy, but also very important. Every couple of hours, two trains would approach the bridge from opposite directions. One would come up the track from Swansea going towards London, and the other would come down the track from London going towards Swansea. On both sides of the bridge there were two sets of tracks, so the trains could pass each other. But over the bridge there was only one set of tracks. When David saw a train approaching, it was his job to pull back one of the levers in his box which would stop one of the trains, allowing the other train to travel safely across the bridge. Then, when that train had passed, he would pull the lever which would move the track and let the other train go across the bridge.

It was a very easy job, but if David fell asleep or wasn't paying attention when the trains came, it could be disastrous. If he forgot to pull the lever, the trains would crash into each other on the bridge.

But the trains never crashed because David took his job very seriously and never fell asleep or forgot to look out for the trains.

Every day David would arrive home from work at 5:30 p.m. He would put the key in the lock and push open the door, and flying towards him came his most favourite person, his son, John. David really loved John. John looked a little bit like his dad. He had blond hair and blue eyes. He was a lot shorter, because John was only four, but apart from that they looked very similar. Every night when David walked through the door John would run across to him, jump into his arms, and yell, "Dad! I've been ever so good today. Ever so good."

David knew that John probably hadn't really been "ever so good" because John was probably the most mischievous four-year-old in the world. One day David had come into the kitchen because he could hear the cat meowing very loudly. He followed the sound into the bathroom and there was John trying to put the cat down the toilet.

"What are you doing, John?" David called.

John smiled at his dad and replied, "Dad, Snowy was dirty so I was washing her."

But that night, just as his dad tucked him into bed, John said, "Dad! I've been ever so good today. Ever so good."

His dad groaned and switched off the light.

On another occasion, David was in the garden painting the fence when John came out to join him. "Can I help, Dad? Blue is my favourite colour. Can I help?" he asked again and again.

His dad knew better and said, "Sorry, John, you can't."

Well, John kept asking and asking and asking again, and eventually added, "Oh, come on, Dad. I'll be ever so good because I'm always ever so good."

David still wouldn't give in. Next door's labrador puppy, whose name was Toby, jumped up at the fence and started barking. "Look, Dad," said John, "even Toby wants me to paint."

John wouldn't give in, so eventually David gave him the paintbrush and said, "I know I'm going to regret this, but I'll let you try. Now, do it slowly and carefully or I'll take the brush from you."

John just laughed. "I'll be good, Dad, because I'm ever so good."

After thirty minutes, John really did look as if he was doing a good job. He painted slowly and carefully and made sure that no drips fell on the grass. John was doing well. So well, in fact, that his dad said, "John, shall I go and make us a cup of tea?"

John said, "OK, Dad. I'll just keep painting because I'm ever so good at this."

David had only been gone for two minutes when he heard Toby barking uncontrollably. David rushed to the garden, but was too late. John was laughing uncontrollably. "Look, dad," he said, pointing to next door's dog. "I've painted Toby."

Sure enough, the golden labrador was blue. John thought it was wonderful. He laughed and laughed and laughed.

But that night, just as his dad tucked him into bed, John said, "Dad! I've been ever so good today. Ever so good."

His dad groaned and switched off the light.

John was always getting into trouble but David couldn't help loving him.

Every morning at 7 a.m. David would sit down to eat his breakfast. John would come down five minutes later still wearing his pyjamas and sit opposite his dad. John would pour his cereal into his bowl – well, some of it went into his bowl, most went on the table. He'd then pour the milk on top. Most of that ended up on the table too. Then he'd look at his dad and say, "Dad, can I come to work with you today?"

David would always say no, but John kept asking.

"Oh, please, Dad. I'll be ever so good."

"No," David would reply. "You have to go to nursery."

John would look at David and say, "But Dad, I don't want to go to school. I want to come to work with you and get money and buy more toys. Can I come, please?"

This happened every single morning. Nag. Nag. Nag. But David wouldn't give in and John had to go to nursery. David refused to give in until one Saturday morning when John came rushing down the stairs and started asking again. David did his best to ignore John. But John asked again, "Dad, can I come?" David said no. John asked and asked and asked again, until at last he said: "Dad, if you let me come to work with you today I'll never ask you ever again for the rest of my life, even when I'm really old like Granny."

David knew he'd regret it, but he gave in. After all, John had promised never to ask again. So he couldn't really miss this opportunity. John couldn't believe it. He rushed upstairs and put his jeans on. Then he remembered he still had his pyjamas on, so he took his jeans off, took his pyjamas off, then put his jeans on and his warm jumper and his big coat and, of course, his green wellington boots. And he was ready to go. So they set off down the street whistling as they went. John really was excited. He was waving to all the neighbours and shouting, "Hello! I'm going to work to get money to buy toys. Hello! I'm going to work and I'm going to be ever so good."

When they eventually arrived at the signal box, David climbed up the ladder first and John followed him. David let John sit in the corner where he could see all the trains go past, and he also gave him some paper and pens to do some colouring.

"I'm ever so good, Dad," John called. "Ever so good."

Nine o'clock came and the train from Swansea went past. All the people were waving and John waved back. And then the London train came and John waved some more. "I'm ever so good, Dad. Ever so good."

Ten o'clock came and the trains went past and "I'm ever so good, Dad. Ever so good."

Eleven o'clock came and the trains went past and "I'm ever so good, Dad. Ever so good."

Twelve o'clock and "I'm ever so good, Dad. Ever so good."

One o'clock and "I'm ever so good, Dad. Ever so good."

Two o'clock and – nothing.

Not a sound.

David looked around and John had gone. He looked out of the window and there was John quite happily playing splash in the puddles by the railway track. After all, he was wearing his green wellies; you have to play splash if you are wearing wellies.

Jump! Splash! Jump! Splash! David banged the window and shouted at John. But John was having too much fun to stop now. This was what green wellies were meant for. Splash! Splash!

Jump! Splash! Jump! Splash! Jump! Oh no, John had got his foot caught in one of the train tracks and couldn't get it free. He pulled and pulled. Then John looked up at his dad and shouted, "Stuck! It's stuck!"

Then John looked down the train track and coming very quickly towards him was the train from Swansea. Then he looked up the track and there was the train coming from London.

John looked up at his dad and screamed, "Stuck! Stuck! Stuck! Stuck!"

There was no way David could get to him in time. David had to make a decision. If he pulled back his lever then the train would go across the bridge safely. But John would be run over. If he didn't pull the lever then lots of people might die but John would be safe. What should he do? Should he let the hundreds of people on the train die and save his son, or should he save all the people and let John die? What a decision.

David decided that he needed to save the people. He pulled the lever and the trains went past. First the London train and they all waved. But nobody saw the tears in David's eyes. Then the Swansea train. But nobody saw the tears in David's eyes. When the trains had gone, David looked down and all that was left was a small green wellington boot still trapped in the tracks.

David stood and cried and cried and cried. Then he heard...

"Dad! Why are you crying?" David turned and looked at John. "Are you crying because I lost my welly?"

David couldn't believe it. "No," he sobbed. "I'm crying because I thought you were dead!"

John thought about this for a while and then said, "I guess that's a good reason to cry."

But that night just as his dad tucked him into bed, John said, "Dad! I've been ever so good today. Ever so good."

Dad groaned and switched off the light.

Elizabeth and
the Aeroplane

Elizabeth was really quite a strange girl to look at. She was seven years old. She always wore big lacy dresses which, even though she was a little bit fat, looked absolutely enormous on her. Her hair was plaited. But instead of hanging down nicely in two plaits, she insisted that the ends were pinned back up into her hair so that she looked like she had two big ears like an elephant.

She was quite unpleasant to know. She never said please or thank you and she always did what she wanted. In fact, she was spoilt. Her dad was a millionaire, and anything she wanted she got. Not by asking, but by demanding.

For the past six months, Elizabeth had been at a boarding school and today she was leaving school to go and see her mum and dad for the summer holidays. She was American, her mum and dad were American, and the boarding school was in England. So it would be quite a journey home.

She had demanded that the housemistress buy her a new white dress, which she was now wearing. So, down the steps she came, wearing the dress. She stopped at the bottom while her chauffeur opened the car door, and in she got. No please or thank you, she simply got in and waited for him to close the door. And off they set for the airport.

At the airport, the chauffeur opened the door and Elizabeth got out of the car and, escorted by a stewardess, walked to her aeroplane. When they arrived at the aeroplane, the stewardess sat Elizabeth in her seat and told her that a food trolley and a drinks trolley would come past at regular intervals and she could have whatever she wanted from the trolleys. And so the plane took off.

After only a couple of minutes the drinks trolley went past.

"Would you like anything?" the stewardess asked.

"Coke, I want Coke," demanded Elizabeth. *Glug, glug, glug!* And it was gone.

Several minutes later the food trolley arrived.

"Would you like anything?" the stewardess asked.

"Peanuts, I want peanuts," demanded Elizabeth. *Crunch, crunch, crunch!* And they were gone.

After a while the drinks trolley was back.

"Would you like anything?" the stewardess asked.

"Coke, I want Coke," demanded Elizabeth again. *Glug, glug, glug!* And it was gone.

It wasn't long until the food trolley arrived again.

"Would you like anything?" the stewardess asked.

"More peanuts. I want peanuts." *Crunch, crunch, crunch.* And they were gone too.

This went on for several hours. Every couple of minutes *glug, glug, glug; crunch, crunch, crunch; glug, glug; crunch, crunch; glug, crunch, glug, crunch.* Loads and loads of peanuts and cans and cans of Coke, all in Elizabeth's tummy.

Now this would have been OK because she had quite a big tummy and it could hold a lot of Coke and peanuts. But the aeroplane went into a storm and the plane started going:

Up and down. Up and down. Up and down...

Now this would have been OK except all the people in the plane started going:

Up and down. Up and down. Up and down...

Now this would have been OK except Elizabeth started going:

Up and down. Up and down. Up and down...

Now this would have been OK except Elizabeth's tummy started going:

Up and down. Up and down. Up and down...

Now even this would have been OK except all the peanuts and Coke inside Elizabeth started going:

Up and down. Up and down. Up and then... OUT!

All over the cabin shot this radioactive, supersonic, turbo-propelled, projectile sick. It left Elizabeth's mouth, it almost broke the sound barrier, it shot down the aeroplane, it knocked a lady's hat off, and hit the end of the cabin so hard the pilot thought he was going to crash.

Elizabeth's white dress was no longer white, it looked more like Joseph's technicolour dreamcoat than it did a white dress. It had greens and yellows and oranges and purples and blues. It was horrible.

Elizabeth had to sit there for another three hours. Eventually the plane landed. Elizabeth got off the plane and started walking towards the main building. When she saw her father, she opened her arms and started running towards him. He was wearing his white shirt. The father saw his little girl running towards him and opened his arms and started running towards Elizabeth. "That's a colourful dress," he thought to himself.

They ran until they were quite close.

"That really is a strange dress," Dad thought.

They came closer and closer and closer, then...

"Aghhh!" Dad saw what was really on the dress and stopped dead.

Elizabeth, however, didn't stop at all but kept running and then jumped up towards her dad's arms, still held wide. Dad was so shocked he just stood there. Closer and closer she flew through the air.

What was Elizabeth's father going to do? Elizabeth soared closer and closer, until eventually she landed right in her dad's arms. *Squelch!* Her father didn't turn her away or move aside. He hugged his little girl close and didn't worry about the dress. He loved his little girl and had missed her so much.

George and Mr Spencer

It came as quite a surprise when George walked into the room and proclaimed, "Mum, Dad, I'm going to be a lawyer and I'm going to Princeton college."

George was born in the state of Georgia in the United States of America. His parents lived on a plantation. The house they owned belonged to a very wealthy man indeed, and they worked for that man and he paid them for their work. They in turn paid rent to that man so that they could live in their house. It was hard work, up every morning at sunrise, out into the fields to plant or to dig or to gather in the crops. They worked through until sunset and returned home to make dinner.

George's mother and father both worked in the fields, and come harvest-time George would help out as well. The people didn't mind working because the owner of the land paid them quite well. Not brilliantly, but well enough to pay rent, buy food and clothes, and sometimes even to buy chocolate.

It hadn't always been this way. George's grandfather had worked the same land but as a slave. He was treated very poorly and was forced to work very hard with no pay at all.

George's mother and father couldn't read. But George knew that if he wanted to do what was in his heart to do then he would have to learn to read. He began to teach himself, and with just a little help from the rich man's daughter who went to a nearby school, he learned to read. But he wanted to do more than read, he wanted to go to Princeton – a very famous college; he wanted to train to become a lawyer. But Princeton cost many thousands of dollars to attend, and George's mum and dad would never have enough money to send him.

George's mum and dad tried to convince him that it was impossible, but he refused to believe them. He was determined. He knew he would never get enough money to go to Princeton by staying on the plantation, so he headed for the city and eventually got a job as a porter on a train. He would carry suitcases on and off the train, collect tickets, show people to their seats – he would do anything to earn more money to pay for his fees when he eventually got to Princeton.

One of the things he would do to try to earn a little more money was to stay up into the early hours of the morning cleaning and polishing people's shoes. He would knock on the doors of the passengers – for George worked on a long-distance train with bedrooms built in – and ask if they needed their shoes polished. He would then work nearly all night polishing shoes – 1 a.m., 2 a.m., 3 a.m., 4 a.m. It may sound an easy job but scraping doggy do-do off shoes was not George's idea of fun. Still, he wanted to go to college and nothing was going to stop him. And at 7 a.m. every morning he would get up and begin his porter work. He worked very hard.

Mr Spencer was a businessman. He travelled on the train very often. But on this particular night he had a lot on his mind. He'd just started a business deal in Chicago and was on his way to New York to complete another deal. It was 2 a.m. in the morning and he couldn't sleep. So he decided to go for a walk. He made his way up the train and saw a light on in the engine room. He looked in. There, sitting on the floor, was George, surrounded by lots of pairs of shoes.

He looked up as Mr Spencer walked in.

"Good evening, sir, or should I say good morning? What brings you up here?"

Mr Spencer explained that he couldn't sleep. He then enquired what George was doing and why. George made Mr Spencer a milky drink and explained how he was working very hard to go to Princeton to train to be a lawyer. Mr Spencer listened intently before he returned to his carriage to go to sleep. That was the last George saw of Mr Spencer.

George worked for another year on that train until eventually he had enough money to pay for the first term's fees. There was no way he could get all the money, but he had enough for the first term. He made an appointment with the head of Princeton college and went to see him.

Most people would have given up many years earlier. Many would never have started. But George knew what he wanted to do and wasn't going to let anyone stop him. It may have seemed impossible but here he was in the office of the head of Princeton.

"You've sent me some money, George," the head began. "But I can't take it."

George began to shake. Had he worked so hard and so long and still he wouldn't be allowed to enter the college? He tried to explain: "I know it's not enough for three years. I know it's not enough for one year. But if you could just let me pay for the first term, then I will go away and earn enough money for the second term and come back again, and then go and earn enough for the third. But please let me start. I've worked so hard…"

The head smiled: "George, I didn't mean you couldn't attend. I meant I couldn't take your money. A year ago a man called Mr Spencer walked into this office and handed me enough money for you to stay in college for three years – until the end of the course – but he said this to me… He said that you were only to have the money if you actually came."

So George began his course at Princeton and four years later he became a lawyer, just as he had always longed to do. Following his successful law career, he became a high court judge, one of the first black men in the USA to do so.

Bushy and Rusty

This is a story about two young foxes. The first was called Rusty. I know that's a strange name, but that's because when he was born his mum and dad looked at him and decided he was the same colour as a rusty old car – so they called him Rusty. The second was called Bushy. I know that name seems even stranger than Rusty, but that's because when he was born his mum and dad saw his tail and decided that it looked as if a large bush had been stuck to his back – so they named him Bushy.

Bushy and Rusty were very good friends. Each day they would meet together after breakfast and go into the meadow to play their favourite games. They would chase each other's tails until they were both very dizzy, and then they'd lie on the ground to catch their breath. Or they would chase the butterflies through the meadow – they could never catch them because butterflies fly too fast, but they liked to run after them just the same.

Rusty was a little bit older than Bushy, so when it came time for the foxes to start school Rusty started school first. Rusty didn't really like school too much because he didn't have any friends there. He tried playing with the squirrels, but that wasn't much fun and he tried playing with the rabbits, but they only wanted to dig holes and bounce about. Rusty was very sad.

Near to Rusty and Bushy's homes was a stream that flowed through the woods, and every evening Rusty would meet his friend Bushy at the side of the stream, and they'd talk about what kind of day it had been. Rusty would tell Bushy how lonely he was and how much he hated school. Bushy tried to cheer Rusty up, but he could see that his friend was really sad.

One day while Rusty was walking around the school playground, feeling very sad and lonely, someone walked up to him and said, "Hey, Rusty, I'd like to be your friend." Well, you would think that Rusty would be happy, but the person who was asking was Walter, a rather naughty weasel. Walter was probably the naughtiest animal in the entire school. He would always talk in class, fight in the playground, and never do what he was told. But Rusty was so lonely and wanted a friend in school so badly that he became Walter Weasel's friend.

After school that day, Rusty told Bushy about his new friend. Bushy wasn't happy at all: "Walter will get you into trouble," he told Rusty. But Rusty didn't listen. He was just glad that he'd found a friend in school.

"Hey, Rusty," said Walter, the next day. "Let's go and throw a stone through Farmer Brown's window."

"We can't do that," replied Rusty. "That would be wrong."

"Are you scared?" asked Walter, with a wicked grin on his face.

"I'm not scared of anything," replied Rusty, who was very scared, but just didn't want to show it.

So Walter and Rusty walked up to Farmer Brown's gate and Walter threw a stone at Farmer Brown's window. SMASH! The window shattered into thousands of little pieces.

"Quick, run!" shouted Walter. The two animals ran away as fast as they could before Farmer Brown had a chance to come out of his house.

Bushy and Rusty

That night, Rusty told Bushy what had happened. Bushy was absolutely furious.

"I told you that Walter would get you into trouble, but you wouldn't listen."

The following day, Walter and Rusty were on their way home from school when Walter said, "Hey Rusty, it's your turn to throw a stone through the window today."

"I can't do that," replied Rusty. "I'm sure it would be wrong."

"Not scared, are you?" Walter asked, with the usual wicked grin on his face.

"I'm not scared of anything," came Rusty's quick reply.

"Then do it!" demanded Walter.

Rusty was more than a little bit scared, he was *very* scared. But he didn't want Walter to know that, so he tiptoed up to the gate, picked up a stone and... SMASH! Straight through the bedroom window. Farmer Brown ran out of his house as fast as he could, but was too late. Walter and Rusty had gone. That night, Bushy couldn't believe what Rusty had done.

"I told you Walter would get you into trouble, but you didn't listen. Now look what's happening."

Bushy was so mad he was shouting at Rusty. But Rusty didn't want to listen. "I don't care," he replied. "Anyway, Walter Weasel's my best friend now and I don't want to see you any more." Bushy was very upset by what Rusty was saying. But there was nothing more he could say, so he walked away with his head held low.

Two weeks later, Rusty and Walter were walking home from school together when Walter turned to Rusty and said: "Let's do something different. Let's sneak out tonight and go and steal a chicken from Father Brown's hen house." Rusty didn't really want to do it, but he didn't want to lose his friend.

That night, Walter and Rusty made their way to Farmer Brown's hen house. When they arrived, Walter said, "OK, Rusty. I'll keep guard and you sneak in and steal a chicken." Rusty was really frightened.

The chickens started clucking and crowing and making all sorts of noises. All the lights went on in the house and Farmer Brown came out as fast as he could, with his gun in his hand. But too late. Walter and Rusty had gone.

Several days passed. Then Walter turned to Rusty and said, "Let's do it again. Let's sneak out tonight and go and steal another chicken from Farmer Brown's hen house." Rusty didn't want to do it, but it was too late, he felt trapped.

That night, Walter and Rusty made their way to Farmer Brown's hen house. When they arrived, Rusty crept up to the hen house, opened the door, grabbed a chicken, and ran out.

The chickens went wild. They started clucking and crowing and making all sorts of noises. All the lights went on in the house and Farmer Brown came out as fast as he could, with his gun in his hand. But too late. Walter and Rusty had gone.

Two days later, Walter turned to Rusty and said, "Let's do it one last time. Let's go and steal one more chicken from Farmer Brown's hen house."

So that night, once again Walter and Rusty made their way to Farmer Brown's hen house. When they arrived, Walter took his usual place on guard outside and Rusty began to make his way into the hen house.

But Farmer Brown was not as stupid as Walter and Rusty thought, and on this night he was hiding behind a tree with his gun in hand. As Rusty began to make his way in, Farmer Brown lifted his gun and aimed it at the hen house door.

Walter saw the gun lifting behind the tree and ran off as fast as he could. Rusty was left in the hen house all alone with Farmer Brown outside. The farmer's finger was on the trigger ready to shoot whoever came out of the hen house.

Bushy and Rusty

Walter had run and run and run as far as he could away from the farmyard.

Bushy was sitting by the stream all by himself. Whoosh! Walter ran past Bushy as fast as his little weasel legs would carry him.

"Walter, where's Rusty?" Bushy shouted. But Walter wasn't going to stop, he just kept running. Bushy knew that Rusty must be in trouble and started to make his way as fast as he could towards Farmer Brown's house.

Meanwhile, Rusty began to make his way towards the hen house door. "Is everything OK, Walter?" Rusty called, very nervously. No reply came. Walter was miles away by now. "Walter, are you there?" Rusty tried again. But no answer came. Rusty began to push the hen house door open with his nose. Farmer Brown got ready to shoot. Rusty opened the door and looked up. His eyes became the size of saucers as he stared straight into Father Brown's gun.

BANG! The gun went off and the smoke began to clear. Farmer Brown picked himself up off the ground and tried to work out what had happened.

Just as Father Brown had pulled the trigger, Bushy had jumped over the fence and straight into him, and the gun had gone off. It had only just missed Rusty!

"Quick, run!" shouted Bushy.

Rusty and Bushy started running towards the woods as fast as they could... BANG! Farmer Brown shot again. But he only managed to hit a nearby tree. BANG! He shot a third time. Too late. The foxes had got away.

When Bushy and Rusty eventually stopped they were exhausted.

Rusty turned to Bushy. He was shaking.

"I'm sorry," he said. "I thought Walter was my friend, but he just got me into trouble and then left me. You are my real friend, Bushy, because you came to help me when I needed you."

Runaway

It was a dark and stormy night. The wind was blowing hard. Flash! And a little later, Boom! The rain kept falling. There was more lightning and more thunder. The wind made strange sounds through the trees. Andrew was soaking. His red T-shirt was so wet it stuck to him. His trainers were making squelching sounds and his jeans had become so tight it was getting very difficult to walk.

Flash! What was that? Andrew was sure he'd seen something move.

He'd heard that there were wolves in this part of the forest. Big wolves with razor-sharp teeth. He was sure that there were eyes staring at him through the darkness. Big, green, glowing eyes. He was cold, lost, and scared. And the eyes seemed to be getting closer.

Andrew didn't have any friends. He had arrived in the forest only the week before and didn't know anybody. He was also quite little. He had been adopted by Mr and Mrs Jones. Andrew had never known his dad, and when he was very, very small, his mum had decided that she didn't want him any more, so she had sent him to an orphanage. He had spent a lot of time crying and a lot of time hoping that his mum would come and collect him, but this didn't happen.

So he stayed in the orphanage for what seemed like ages until Mr and Mrs Jones came and asked if they could adopt him.

"Nobody wants me," he would say to himself. "My mother didn't want me, I haven't got any friends, and now I'm living in a strange house with Mr and Mrs Jones."

Mr and Mrs Fox had one other son. His name was Robert. Robert was slightly older than Andrew, and he didn't really know if he was happy having another boy in his house. It meant that he would have to share his bedroom. "Well," he said to himself. "I'll share my bedroom, but I'm not sharing my toys."

One day, it was raining outside. Andrew didn't have any toys of his own, and he was bored. He looked out of the window at the rain falling and the trees blowing in the wind. "I know," he thought. "I'll play with some of Robert's toys. He's not around. It'll be OK." And that's when Robert walked in, and there was Andrew playing with his train set.

Robert got very angry and shouted at Andrew, "You leave my train set alone! It's not yours, it's mine. You don't even belong here. You're only here because no one else wanted you."

Andrew ran out of the room, crying. He ran into the hallway and he was running so fast that even when he saw Mrs Jones in front of him he couldn't stop. He knocked Mrs Jones over.

"Andrew, watch where you're going!" she shouted. And then, "Andrew, stop. What's wrong?"

Andrew ran to the front door, still crying. He slammed the door and ran out into the rain. He kept on running deeper and deeper into the forest. And that's where he was now. Deep in the middle of the forest – and lost.

He was sure there was something walking towards him. Flash! More lightning, but this time he definitely caught a glimpse of a creature. It was very big with large teeth and huge eyes. It was a wolf, and it was getting closer.

Andrew was very frightened. He didn't know much about God. He knew that Mr and Mrs Jones went to church a lot, but he'd only been once. Still, he was very scared and began to pray: "God, help me!"

Flash! Another flash of lightning. The wolf was only metres away. Andrew was shaking. He was sure that he was going to get eaten.

The wolf came closer.

But what was that? Lights! One torch, and then another. Suddenly there seemed to be lots of them. And Andrew could hear his name being called.

"Oh! They're looking for me. I didn't think anyone would come. I didn't think anyone wanted me."

The wolf came even closer.

"Andrew, where are you?"

The wolf looked up and saw that he was outnumbered. He snarled at Andrew before he turned and ran back into the deeper forest.

"I'm here!" Andrew shouted.

There must have been over twenty torches now. Everyone had come looking for Andrew. Mr Jones was the first to arrive. He rushed to Andrew and said, "Thank God you're alive."

Robert came soon after. He hung his head as he said, "I'm sorry. I thought my mum and dad would stop loving me when you came, and would love you instead. But now I know that they love us both. I'm special because I was born into the family, but you're *really* special because Mum and Dad actually chose you."

Andrew began to cry, not with sad tears, but with tears of joy. He'd never felt wanted before. He'd never felt he belonged before. They took him back to the house, and after a warm bath and some milk, he went to bed in his new home with his new brother and new mum and dad.

Samantha

"When the horn blows, all you have to do is follow the rest of the foxhounds and run up the track. Have you got that?" Giles asked.

Samantha nodded.

Samantha the foxhound puppy was very excited. This was the first time she had been on a fox hunt. Giles, the kennel man, was in charge of all the dogs and he'd spent a lot of time explaining to her what to do.

"When the horn blows, all you have to do is follow the rest of the foxhounds."

It was all very straightforward. But Giles was always a little concerned about Samantha. The horn blew and the hunt was on. The other dogs straightened their legs. Samantha straightened her legs. The other dogs stuck their tails in the air. Samantha stuck her tail in the air. The other dogs started running up the track after the horses. Samantha started running… straight through the hedge and into the field.

Samantha knew that she was supposed to follow the other dogs, but she didn't much feel like following today, and anyway she had smelt something interesting through the hedge. She sniffed her way through the long grass and eventually found her nose pushing against someone else's nose. She lifted up her head, and there facing her was a small fox.

"Who are you?" asked Samantha

"My name is Little Jay. I'm a fox cub," the fox replied, politely. "And who are you?"

"My name is Samantha. I'm a foxhound."

The two animals looked at each other curiously for some time. Samantha began to think. She was sure she was supposed to know something about foxes. Fox. Foxhound. Fox. Foxhound. Fox. Foxhound...

"I know!" she said at last. "We must be related, cousins or something. That's it. Cousins."

Little Jay agreed. "I'm sure you are right." So they began jumping and running and chasing and having the most wonderful time. Just then, Mrs Fox returned and, seeing the foxhound, she was very worried. She knew that foxhounds sometimes killed foxes. She shouted to Little Jay: "Little Jay, come away at once."

Little Jay didn't understand, he was having a great time, but he listened to his mum and wandered away. It was then that Samantha realized she was alone. She didn't know her way back and began to cry. Mrs Fox looked at her. She knew that Samantha was very young and couldn't hurt her or Little Jay. She felt sorry for her.

"Follow me," she shouted.

Samantha followed Mrs Fox, who led her all the way back to the farmhouse where Samantha lived. Samantha began to run down the hill to the farmhouse when she realized that she hadn't said thank you to Mrs Fox. She turned around but both the foxes had gone. Samantha rushed down the hill, very happy about meeting a new friend. She ran all the way to the bottom. She was going so fast she couldn't stop, and BASH! She ran right into Giles. He was very angry and would surely have scolded her if Lucy, Giles's daughter, hadn't stopped him.

Samantha

"Be kind to her," she said. "She's only young."

"Young she may be," replied Giles, "but she had better learn fast. She will be the leader of the pack one day."

Samantha was confused. She didn't know what a leader was. How could she be one if she didn't know what one was?

Spring came to an end, the summer came, then the autumn, and the start of winter. It was time to go fox hunting again.

"Now listen to me, Samantha. When that horn blows, you must follow those other foxhounds," Giles gave his usual speech. "All you have to do is follow the rest. It is really rather simple."

The horn blew and the hunt was on. The other dogs straightened their legs. Samantha straightened her legs. The other dogs stuck their tails in the air. Samantha stuck her tail in the air. The other dogs started running up the track after the horses. Samantha started running up the track after the horses. The other dogs started to sniff the ground, looking for the right smell. Samantha started to sniff the ground.

It was all going really well. Giles was delighted, and then... Samantha realized what she could smell. It was Little Jay. These dogs were hunting Little Jay! Well, they might be hunting Little Jay but there was no way she was going to hunt her friend. She turned around and ran back to the farm.

Giles was furious: "Samantha, where are you going? You are a foxhound. Foxhounds hunt foxes."

Samantha lay down on the ground as if to say, "Other foxhounds may hunt foxes, but not this foxhound."

Giles took her by the collar and tied her to the gate with a big rope.

"There you will stay until you learn to hunt foxes," he said.

Samantha sat down. If she had to stay here until she agreed to hunt her friend, then Samantha was going to stay here for a long, long time. There she sat for many weeks. Giles brought her food and water and asked her every day if she was ready to hunt foxes. But every day she just looked at the ground.

She would have undoubtedly stayed there a lot longer but one very special day, Lucy decided that she would sneak Samantha out so she could visit London. She undid the rope and quietly smuggled Samantha into the back of the car. They drove to London. Samantha found London very exciting, but she didn't like being tied up outside of the shops when Lucy went in them. She was getting bored. So, when Lucy went into the next shop, she decided to go exploring. Lucy hadn't tied her up very tightly, so she easily wriggled free and made her way down the street. It wasn't long before she came to a rather curious looking road. She looked up at the sign. It said "Downing Street".

"This is a strange street," thought Samantha. "Why does it have these iron bars? And why are all these policemen here?"

Samantha began to make her way up the street. She came to a big door with two policemen outside.

"I wonder what's in there?" she thought. "I'll go and look."

And as quick as a flash, she shot past the policemen and straight into the house.

"STOP!" shouted the policemen, who started running after Samantha.

Samantha ran over the chairs, up the stairs, under the bed, back down the stairs and out of the back gate, and straight into the strangest-looking dog she had ever seen. It looked as if the dog had run into a wall and squashed his nose flat.

"Who are you?" asked Samantha

"I'm Barney. I'm a bulldog. But not just any bulldog. I belong to the prime minister."

Samantha knew she should be impressed, but she simply wasn't. For one thing, dogs with flat noses didn't impress her, and for another, she had no idea what a prime minister was.

"What's a prime minister?" she asked. Barney couldn't believe that Samantha had never heard of the prime minister. He tried to explain.

"He leads the country."

"What's leading?" asked Samantha.

This was hard to explain, but eventually Barney said, "Well, a leader makes the decisions. A leader decides where to go, and people follow them."

Samantha understood. But she didn't have a chance to talk further because the policemen eventually caught up with her, took her by the collar and led her to the front door, down the street, and handed her back to Lucy, who was waiting for her. All the way back home, Samantha just lay on her tummy and thought hard. She thought about what a leader was. She remembered Barney's words: "A leader decides where to go, and people follow them."

She made a decision. She had an idea. She had a plan. When they arrived home, Lucy tied Samantha back up. Giles didn't even know she had gone.

The next day, when Giles brought Samantha her food, he asked the usual question: "Samantha, are you ready to hunt foxes now?"

This time, to Giles's surprise, Samantha started barking frantically. He untied the rope. And over the next couple of weeks Samantha practised her running until she could run faster than all the other dogs. She practised her jumping until she could jump further than all the other dogs. And she practised her sniffing until she could smell smells that none of the other dogs could smell.

It was the day of the next fox hunt. Giles was delivering his usual speech: "So, when the horn blows, all you have to do is follow the rest of the foxhounds and run up the track. Have you got that? Just follow," repeated Giles.

The horn blew and the hunt was on. The other dogs straightened their legs. Samantha straightened her legs. The other dogs stuck their tails in the air. Samantha stuck her tail in the air. The other dogs started running up the track after the horses. Samantha started running up the track after the horses. The other dogs started to sniff the ground, looking for the right smell. Samantha started to sniff the ground.

It was all going really well.

"Just follow the rest," Giles shouted.

But to Giles's amazement, that was the last thing that Samantha intended. As soon as she found the smell that she was looking for, she set off. She was now the fastest of the dogs, so she soon took the lead. She ran and leapt and sniffed. She wasn't going to follow. Today she was going to lead. She led them over fields, through clumps of trees, through streams, over and through hedges; they ran and ran and ran. And when they couldn't run any further, she led them home again.

That day everyone had a great time. The horses, the dogs, the riders – and now that Samantha was the leader, even the fox had a nice day. For Little Jay had sat on the hillside watching the whole thing. And Samantha knew where he was, too. She had led the hunt everywhere except where the foxes were. She refused to follow. She would lead. And when you are the leader you get to decide where to go, and others follow.

Whether you are a good leader or not depends where you are leading. Samantha had become a good leader.

Carlos

Carlos sat down in his bedroom and looked around the sea of beds in the dormitory. There were fifteen beds in all. It was crowded but comfortable. All the boys who shared the dormitory had their own cupboard for storing their things – not that Carlos had many things. He had two pairs of trousers that had been given to him, two T-shirts, a jumper, and a sprinkling of underwear and socks. Oh, and the coat that one of the older boys had kindly given him because it didn't fit any longer.

Carlos looked into the mirror fastened to his cupboard. He stared. Two bright blue eyes stared back. He began to get ready for bed. He put on his boxer shorts and looked at himself in the mirror one more time. He was hoping that his muscles would arrive soon, but there didn't seem to be any signs yet. He flexed his left arm, but there really was nothing there. Nothing except Carlos's strange mark. On the top of his left arm there was a very curious shape. It looked liked a wave splashing onto the shore. Carlos had often wondered what it was, but recently had decided it was just a birthmark.

Carlos crawled into bed and lay back on his pillow. He pushed his long curly blond hair out of his eyes and stared up at the ceiling.

Carlos was nine years old. The place he lived in may not be his real home, but it felt like home to him. He grabbed his stuffed rabbit that by now was looking a bit worse for wear. He snuggled it under his chin.

Carlos's earliest memories were very happy ones. He remembered being rocked to sleep by his father; he remembered the feel of the cot blankets on his face. His fondest memories were of looking up into his mother's radiant blue eyes as she sang to him a song of cows jumping over moons and of plates running away with spoons. The little stuffed rabbit was his only reminder of that time. Somehow that world had vanished and now he lived with many other boys and girls in an orphanage run by monks. Carlos lay on his bed little realizing that everything was about to change.

Carlos often thought about where he had come from. The monks had told him of how they had found him on the steps outside the orphanage, wrapped in a blue woollen blanket with "Carlos" embroidered on it and clutching his stuffed rabbit. He had been about eighteen months old. Carlos celebrated his birthday on 1 January, but he wasn't quite sure how the monks knew when his birthday was. Whenever he had asked them he was told that they had guessed, but Carlos felt that they were hiding something. Carlos had always felt that they were hiding something.

Carlos thought about his parents often. He asked himself again and again why they would leave him on the steps of the monastery. He remembered when he was little how he had thought that it must have been his fault. "Maybe it was because they thought I was ugly," he'd said to himself. "Maybe I did something to upset them. Maybe they never really wanted me." He remembered the agonizing times when his mind was full of the question "WHY?". He had spent many tearful nights and still more tearful days trying to work it out. But he had discovered when he had explained how he felt to God in prayer – as the monks showed him – he did feel better. And slowly but surely he had begun to realize that it couldn't possibly have been his fault – after all, he was so young. And another thing, every time he remembered being with his parents he could only remember happy times. He was sure his mother and father had loved him dearly.

Eventually Carlos let all the bad feelings he had fade away. He asked God to help him and he tried to remember the happy times. So now when Carlos lay thinking about those times he only felt happy feelings – and, of course, curiousity. He wondered who he really was and where he had really come from. He couldn't help feeling that maybe he was a bit special. His eyes became heavy and eventually he dropped off to sleep.

It was New Year's Eve and the day before Carlos's birthday. Birthdays weren't a big thing at the orphanage, too many of the children there had no idea when they were born, so the whole thing was played down. Nobody seemed particularly excited by the fact that they were entering a new year, either. Everyone slept. The orphanage was peaceful, until…

It sounded like an explosion. There was fire sweeping up the walls of the orphanage. Carlos opened his eyes. There was chaos. There were men walking around the dormitory with masks on. They were asking the boys questions. They were searching. They were looking for somebody. Carlos heard one of the men asking where Carlos was. They were looking for Carlos!

Carlos rolled off the bed and scrambled underneath. He waited until one of the men had walked past and then he scurried into his cupboard and closed the door. He could just make out what was happening from a small crack. The orphanage was clearly on fire, but the men weren't trying to leave. They had lined all the boys up beside their beds and were asking them where Carlos was. Then the monks were brought in and asked the same question. They all answered truthfully, "We don't know. He should have been in his bed."

But the men weren't satisfied. They began to shout that the monks were hiding him, and one of the monks was knocked to the ground. Carlos thought the monks would be shot but the man who was clearly the leader ordered that all the monks and all the children be removed and taken back to the castle. Then one by one they were marched out. By now the flames had engulfed most of the orphanage, and Carlos felt that he would be burned alive.

Carlos waited as long as he could. Then, coughing and spluttering, he burst out of the cupboard. He didn't really know why, but he made a special point of grabbing his old stuffed rabbit – and a blanket. He rushed out of the room and down the stairs to the ground floor, but ahead of him the front door seemed obliterated by flames.

Carlos waited, then covering himself with the blanket, he ran towards the front door. He burst through the door into the garden. He rolled on the ground to make sure all the flames were out, and then pulled the blanket off. He was unharmed, but very shaken.

Carlos turned to see the orphanage behind him. It lit up the night sky. He stood astounded. He didn't know what to do. He was alone. The monks had been taken away.

Carlos felt deserted yet again. He began to feel as he had done before. He started to think that this was all his fault. After all, it was definitely him these men were looking for. His mum and dad had deserted him, and now the orphanage had been destroyed. Maybe Carlos made bad things happen.

Then Carlos stopped himself thinking those things. He knew that it wasn't true. Something inside told him that he was special, that he was important, and even though he felt separated and alone right now, he knew it wasn't his fault. He would have to sort all this out. He would have to find the monks, and maybe in doing so he might find out who he really was. The monks' trail wouldn't be difficult to follow, there were countless footprints going into the desert. He would track them down.

Carlos

Carlos set out. He walked into the night with countless thoughts flying through his head. He kept walking, following the tracks of the masked men until he could see lights in the distance. It was a village, a village almost in the heart of the desert. He knocked on the first door to ask if the masked men had come this way, but he was so tired. He fell through the door as it opened and lay exhausted on floor.

The next thing he knew, he was gazing up into the eyes of a very kind-looking lady. She was offering him soup, which he willingly took. He was beginning to feel that he had no chance of rescuing the others. And anyway, who did he think he was to be able to rescue his friends and the monks from those masked men?

Carlos finished his soup. He felt better. His rabbit still lay beside him. He stood up and walked to a washbasin nearby. He poured some water into the bowl and splashed it onto his face. He took off his top and began to wash himself. The lady returned, collected his bowl, and was about to leave when she saw the mark on his arm – his birthmark. She let out a scream and dropped the bowl. It smashed and brought the rest of the family running in – two men and two teenage boys stood staring at Carlos. Then they dropped to their knees. Carlos didn't understand. He didn't know what was going on. Then the oldest man looked up at Carlos and proclaimed, "You are Prince Carlos. You are the son of the king who was killed by the masked men."

The next couple of hours became a blur for Carlos. Very soon the whole village seemed to be outside his door. Then even more people came, then others. Word was spreading to other villages in the desert that the new king had come. Carlos was dressed in the finest clothes and many people clamoured to bring him gifts. They were bowing low and bringing him present upon present. It was quite a new experience for someone who had never received a present in his life – apart from his stuffed rabbit.

The elders of each of the villages were called, and came to stand before Carlos. They all agreed that he was the rightful king. They could not deny the birthmark. Also, most of them remembered the old king and said that Carlos looked just like him. They were prepared to make Carlos king in an official ceremony. He could live in the best house – they apologized for not being able to put him in the castle, but the masked men had captured it the same night that Carlos's parents had been killed.

Carlos listened carefully. He knew that he would be able to live the rest of his life having whatever he wanted, with servants and gifts and nice clothes and lovely food. But he also remembered the monks that had taken care of him, and also his friends. And, of course, there was the fact that these masked men had killed his parents and were now living in his castle. He had been rescued, but he was going to become the rescuer.

He told the elders of each village what he wanted to do. They looked very nervous, but how could they disobey their king? They each summoned their fighting men and made their way to fight against the masked men. They marched all day and camped outside the castle at dusk. The night was spent listening to the laughter and jokes from the masked men who stood on the battlements. Clearly they didn't think Carlos's army a threat at all.

The following morning, Carlos's men prepared for battle. They stood in battle formation and awaited orders. The masked men, instead of staying in the castle and waiting for the attack, opened the drawbridge and charged. Carlos was amazed – the masked men were so confident of victory they didn't fight from the castle. Carlos gave the order to charge. But the masked men were superior warriors. They chopped men down from their lofty camels; they wiped out over a hundred of them. Then they returned to their castle to once again stand on the battlements and laugh and joke.

Carlos didn't know what to do. He became angry with himself. How could he have thought that he could gain the victory over such superior forces? How could he have been so full of pride? He picked up his little stuffed rabbit and hurled it at a nearby rock, in frustration. But the rabbit, instead of thudding against the rock, made a rattling sound. Carlos examined the rabbit. He borrowed a knife, cut a small hole at the bottom of the stuffed rabbit, and rummaged until he found an iron key. He pulled it out and stared at it. He could see that some of the others were staring at it too.

One of the eldest men walked up and looked at the key. He smiled. "Carlos, you have the key to the castle."

Carlos couldn't believe it. He arranged his men for ambush, and they crept into the castle in the middle of the night. The masked men were brave warriors, but they were taken by surprise. Carlos's men took all the masked men without a fight.

Carlos set his friends free. Many of them stayed and lived in the castle with Carlos. The monks returned to their monastery. The rescued had become the rescuer.

Starfish

There's a certain beach in Australia where once a year something truly amazing happens. They have a very high tide, which means that the sea comes up a very long way. And when the sea returns to its normal position it leaves hundreds of starfish trapped on the beach.

On one of these occasions, a young boy came onto the beach and started picking up the starfish one by one and throwing them back into the water.

After a while, an old man appeared and saw what the little boy was doing. He walked up behind the boy, stood nearby, and watched for a while.

"What are you doing that for, you silly boy?" he croaked.

"I'm saving the starfish," the little boy replied.

"You really are a silly boy," the old man said, with a little laugh. "You'll never get them all. There are hundreds of starfish on this beach."

The little boy smiled, picked up a starfish, and holding up it up to the man, said, "Mister, I may never be able to save all these starfish, but I can save this one."

With that, the little boy took the starfish and threw it back into the sea.

Maisie's Birthday Party

It was the night before Maisie's birthday party and she was very excited.

She paced up and down the house, sat down, stood up, sat down again. She was so excited she couldn't wait for her birthday to come. She was so looking forward to her birthday that as soon as it was six o'clock, off she went to bed. Her mum said, "It's too early to go to bed."

But Maisie was so excited she figured if she went to bed early, then the morning would come quicker and she'd get her birthday presents quicker. She lay in her bed. Do you think she could sleep? No, she couldn't. She turned this way, then that way. She tried sleeping where her feet should be, she tried sleeping without the duvet, and she tried sleeping without her pillow. She just couldn't get to sleep.

At eleven o'clock, when her mum and dad went to bed, she was still awake. She tried and tried to sleep but she was just too excited. She could hear Dad snoring.

Eventually at about two in the morning, she fell asleep. Soon, it was the next morning and she was awake and very, very excited. She rushed to the bottom of the stairs and straight to the front door to look for the cards the postman would surely have delivered.

Nothing!

She didn't worry. She thought: "Mum must have taken them and left them on the table with my presents."

She rushed into the kitchen. There was Dad eating his breakfast, there was Mum eating her breakfast, and the dog was eating his breakfast too. But where were her cards, where were her presents? Nowhere to be seen. She sat down but nobody said "Happy Birthday".

Eventually Maisie set off for school, feeling a little bit fed up.

"Never mind," she thought, "at least my friends in school will remember my birthday."

Maisie arrived at school and started to walk into the playground. But nobody said "Happy Birthday", nobody gave her any cards. Her best friend, Jane, asked her if she wanted to play, but not even she said "Happy Birthday".

Her teacher didn't say "Happy Birthday". Her headmaster didn't say "Happy Birthday". Nobody said "Happy Birthday". They'd all forgotten.

Eventually she thought, "Maybe they've arranged a surprise party for me after school, and they're all keeping it a secret."

At home time, Maisie rushed off as fast as she could. But when she arrived, everyone had got there before her. All her friends were there. Her mum and dad were there. But Maisie couldn't believe what she was seeing. Everyone was giving presents to everyone else, but nobody was giving presents to Maisie. Everyone had forgotten her birthday. Maisie couldn't believe it. She stood on the kitchen table and began to shout, "What about me? What about me? It's my birthday! What about me? What about me? What about me? What about me? What about me?"

The next thing Maisie felt was somebody shaking her. "Maisie, wake up, wake up. You're having a bad dream."

Maisie's Birthday Party

It was her dad. Maisie had been dreaming it all. It was only midnight and her birthday hadn't even arrived.

When she got up in the morning and went to the front door, there were loads of cards for her. Mum and Dad gave her presents, and there was even one from the dog. All her friends in school said "Happy Birthday", as did the teacher and headmaster. And when she got home that night there was a special party just for her.

She went to bed that night feeling very, very happy.

Harvey's Little Sister

Mrs Thompson prayed every day for all the children in her class, but she prayed especially hard for Harvey.

Harvey was the class leader. He was the person that everyone else in the class followed. He was the person that set an example for everyone else, and most of the rest of the class did as he did. When the class made a visit to Salisbury to see Stonehenge, he was the person who had jumped over the fence to get a better look at the stones – and the rest of the class had followed him. There was nothing wrong with Harvey being the leader, but Mrs Thompson prayed that Harvey would learn to be a good example.

Mrs Thompson knew that God always heard her prayers, but she didn't realize that God had decided to show Harvey just how important it was to set a good example. God would let Harvey see for himself how sad it could be when he set a bad example.

It happened one weekend.

Harvey had rushed home from school on Friday evening. He had spent the entire evening sorting out his bag, his rod, his bait, his nets, his sandwiches... Tomorrow he was going fishing. He'd heard the weatherman say it was going to be sunny, so he was going down to the river and he was going to catch lots of fish, and lie in the sun and have a nice time. He went to bed and slept very well. He was up at 7 a.m. and ready for fishing. Then it happened, the disaster hit.

He was just finishing his breakfast when his mum came downstairs and asked, "Where are you going so early, Harvey?"

"Fishing, Mum. It's a perfect day for it," he replied.

"Oh no, you are not! We told you months ago that your father and I had a trip to London planned for today, and you were to look after Sophie."

Harvey couldn't believe it. He knew his mum was right, but he'd forgotten about it. This was going to be such a good day, and now he was going to spend it trapped in the house with his whirlwind little sister. It wasn't that he didn't love his sister. He really did. But she was always sneaking into his room and playing with his computer, or messing up his books, or hanging around him like a shadow.

Sophie didn't mean to be a nuisance. She just loved her brother and wanted to be with him all the time. Several times Mrs Thompson had had to send her back to her own classroom because she wanted to stay in Harvey's class. Of course, Sophie couldn't stay in Harvey's class; she was only four and was supposed to be in the nursery class. But she did so love her brother.

Well, there it was, whether Harvey liked it or not, he was looking after his sister for the day. Sophie didn't get up until 9 a.m., by which time Harvey's parents had left. But she was looking forward to having a fun day with her brother. She was dressed in her favourite yellow T-shirt, her dungarees, and her little pink trainers.

"Hi, Harvey! What are we going to do today?"

It was then that Harvey had the idea. Maybe he didn't have to stay in the house. Maybe he could take Sophie fishing. He knew she'd scare the fish, but at least it was better than being in the house all day.

"Eat your breakfast, Sophie. We're going fishing."

Sophie crinkled up her face. "Are you sure, Harvey? Mummy says that I shouldn't go near the river."

"She means by yourself," said Harvey. "You'll be OK with me. Come on, eat up."

Just after 10 a.m. Harvey and Sophie set off for the river. Harvey was carrying the fishing rod, sandwiches, and a big blanket. Sophie was carrying a really heavy bucket with a lid on it. She didn't know what was in the bucket. Harvey wouldn't tell her. Harvey hadn't told her because if Sophie had found out she was carrying a bucket full of worms she would never have agreed to carry it. At 11:30 a.m. they arrived at the riverbank. Harvey put down the big blanket and took the lid off the bucket, much to Sophie's horror. He began to get his fishing rod ready. Sophie didn't have a fishing rod, but she so wanted to be like her brother that she got a stick, got some string out of her pocket, tied it to the stick, and pretended to fish as well.

It really was going nicely. By 1 p.m. Harvey had caught five fish and Sophie hadn't scared any of them away. But by 2 p.m. Sophie was getting hot. It was a beautiful day. The sun shone down, the birds sang in the trees, butterflies flew past. But Sophie was thirsty, and although Harvey had brought sandwiches which they'd eaten before midday, he'd forgotten about drinks. By 2:30 p.m. Sophie was unbearable. Harvey knew that he'd have to get something to drink. There was a shop not too far away on the other side of the river. There was a bridge, but that was a long way upstream. Harvey knew there was another way across. There was an old waterpipe which stretched across the river. It wasn't very thick, but Harvey had balanced across it before. He told Sophie to stay where she was, to sit and watch the rod and not to go anywhere until he came back. Then he set off.

Sophie watched in amazement as Harvey balanced on the pipe. She was so proud of her brother. She thought he could do anything. Harvey kept his balance across to the other side and went to the shop. The sign on the door said: "Back in five minutes."

Harvey waited. Sophie waited as well, wondering where her brother was. Ten minutes later the shopkeeper eventually came back, and Harvey bought the cans of drink. But Sophie had got tired of waiting. She had walked to the waterpipe and looked across the river.

"Surely I can do this," she thought to herself. It must be OK. After all, Harvey had done it. She put one foot onto the pipe and then the other foot. She was balancing on the pipe…

Harvey walked back from the shop quickly. He didn't like leaving his sister alone for so long. But he wasn't ready for the sight that greeted him when he arrived at the waterpipe. Sophie was balancing on the pipe. She lifted up her head and saw Harvey coming and shouted, "Harvey! Look at me. I'm doing what you did. I'm just like you, Harvey."

But just then, to Harvey's horror, Sophie lost her balance! With a scream, Harvey's little four-year-old sister tumbled head first into the river and was pulled downstream. Harvey dropped the cans and ran along the side of the bank, shouting.

Sophie disappeared under the water.

"Sophie! Where are you?" Harvey screamed.

It seemed like for ever before her head popped back up.

"Harvey, help me!" Sophie shouted.

Harvey dived. He swam with all his might towards his little sister.

"Hold on, Sophie, I'm coming."

Harvey swam like he'd never swum before, until he eventually grabbed his little sister. He pulled her head out of the water and held on tight. He hadn't thought what he would do next. He just wanted to save his sister. Anything might have happened if an old fisherman hadn't seen them. He quickly grabbed a round life buoy from the side of the river and threw it towards Harvey.

"Catch this!" he yelled.

Harvey grabbed at it. He missed. He tried again and again. Then he had it. He held tight as he and Sophie were pulled to safety. The fisherman drove them straight home, just in time to meet their parents who had just come home.

They had a lot of explaining to do, but at least they were safe. And Harvey had learnt an important lesson about being a leader.

Donna, Darren, and Daniel

Donna, Darren, and Daniel Tompkins were triplets. They were all born on 7 June. They were all eight years old. Every day their mother would wake them up for school: "Come on, Donna, come on, Darren, and come on, Daniel."

They would all make their way downstairs for breakfast. They all had cereal. And then they put on some warm clothes, ready to walk to school.

They all put on bright red wellington boots, green mittens, blue scarves, striped bobble hats and then, if it was raining, they all put on their bright yellow raincoats, and off they went to school.

When they arrived in school they all made their way to Mrs Smith's class. They took off their coats, scarves, hats, and mittens, and sat down. They were all the same age, they all lived in the same house, they all ate the same things, they all dressed the same, and they were all in the same class. But they certainly never behaved the same.

At 9:30 a.m. Mrs Smith said, "Excuse me for a while. I've got to step out of the room for ten minutes. Can I trust you to carry on with your work quietly until I return?"

They all replied, "Yes, Miss."

As soon as she was out of the room, Darren started shouting: "Hey! Steven, what's the answer for number 7? Jamie, do you want to come and play football with me later? Becky, what a horrible dress!"

Donna tried to make Darren stop, but he didn't listen and kept shouting: "What's the answer to number 7? Come on, somebody tell me."

Just then, Mrs Smith walked back in, but Darren didn't see her and kept shouting: "What's the answer for number 7? Come on, Becky. I'll give you 50p if you..." Darren lifted his eyes and looked straight up at Mrs Smith, who was standing over him, not looking particularly happy. Darren started: "Hi, Miss. I was just telling the class to stop talking but they wouldn't listen."

Mrs Smith didn't believe him and simply said: "Darren, I'm very disappointed that I couldn't trust you in such a small thing."

At 10:15 a.m. it was time for assembly. Mrs Smith said, "Can I trust you all to behave during assembly, and not talk, and to sit still?"

They all replied, "Yes, Miss."

Darren was made to sit by Mrs Smith so he couldn't get into any more trouble. Donna talked to her friend Lisa right the way through assembly. And halfway through she started kicking Steven in the back until he began to cry.

On the way back to class, Mrs Smith called Donna to her and said: "Donna, I'm very disappointed in you. I asked you to do such a small thing and I couldn't even trust you to do that."

At lunchtime Darren climbed up a tree – which he knew was wrong. He got stuck and a dinner lady had to come and help him down. Donna actually got into a fight and was sent to stand in the hall by herself.

Daniel played football and behaved very well.

After lunch, Mrs Smith told Darren and Donna how disappointed she was in them.

Donna, Darren, and Daniel

At 2:30 p.m. Mrs Smith said, "I've got a special announcement to make. Next week the Queen is coming to our village, and our school has been asked to go and meet her. Out of the whole school, our class will get to shake her hand. And out of the whole class, one person has been chosen to present her with a bunch of flowers."

Do you think it was Donna, Darren, or Daniel?

I'm Not Forgiving Them

Karen and Nigel were husband and wife, and they loved each other very much. They had been married for five years when Arthur was born. When baby Arthur was first born, his mum and dad loved him a lot. They would take him shopping and to the zoo, to the beach, and to the funfair. They loved him so much. They also loved each other a lot.

But when Arthur was seven, his mum and dad began to argue. And when Arthur was nine, Dad came to him one day and said, "Arthur, I can't stay anymore. I'm leaving. Please forgive me." And Dad walked off, leaving Mum and Arthur by themselves.

Now Arthur, of course, had two choices. He could forgive his dad – after all, he did say sorry – or he could decide not to. Arthur was hurt on the inside and he couldn't forgive. He felt too sad. And so his heart felt heavy, as if a heavy weight had been placed in it. It wasn't Arthur's fault that Dad left. He thought it was, for a while, but he knew that he hadn't done anything wrong. But this big heavy weight was also making Arthur different. He knew it was.

I'm Not Forgiving Them

Only a few days after his dad left, his friend Harry asked to borrow his pencil, and Arthur got angry. He shouted at Harry, "Buy your own!" It wasn't really like Arthur, but the heavy weight in his heart was making him mean, sour, and very sad. He was very unhappy and he was getting angrier. He was getting into fights and misbehaving, and was ending up in all sorts of trouble.

It was six months later that everything changed. A girl from his class called Rosie was waiting for him by the school gates. He was walking towards her, alone. He walked to lots of places alone now. His anger was turning all his friends away. They didn't really want to be with Arthur. But Rosie waited. When Arthur arrived, she asked if she could talk to him. He shrugged and said he didn't care, but she tried anyway.

"Arthur, you know we all like you and we all used to be really good friends. Well, you're being really unfriendly and if you keep this up, nobody will want to be with you anymore."

Arthur shrugged again and told Rosie he didn't care. But Rosie knew that he did. She continued, "Three years ago, Arthur, my mum left and now she's married to someone called Jack. Don't you think I felt angry? Don't you think I wanted to be cross all the time? But I worked it out. I was only hurting myself. Nobody else. My friends tried to help and I pushed them away. But I worked it out. I had to forgive."

Arthur started, "But... but..." He wanted to be cross, he wanted to shout at Rosie. But he also knew she was right and she wouldn't say these things if she didn't care. And now tears began to run down his cheeks. He tried his best to wipe them away, and Rosie tried her best to pretend they weren't there.

Arthur cried a lot that night and eventually phoned his dad the following morning to say he forgave him. Dad sounded half asleep and very confused. But Arthur wasn't really doing it for Dad, he was doing it for himself. He needed to get rid of that heavy weight on his heart, and forgiveness was the only solution.

It still hurt and he still cried sometimes, but the weight in his heart had gone.

It's hard to forgive, sometimes. But if we don't forgive it's like we carry that heavy weight in our hearts. Some people never forgive and they carry that weight all their lives. But Arthur was very courageous and forgave. Rosie was also courageous. She found talking to Arthur really hard, and it was even harder talking about her mum and Jack, but she knew that talking to her friend about the hard stuff showed that they were *real* friends.

Telemachus and the Gladiators

This story is about a man who lived nearly two thousand years ago – a man called Telemachus. Not only did he have a peculiar name, he also had a peculiar job. Telemachus was a monk.

One day, Telemachus visited the great city of Rome. Rome was usually a very noisy city where thousands of people walked the streets and where children played all sorts of exciting games. Today Rome was silent. The streets were deserted. As Telemachus made his way through the streets, he wondered where all the people had gone. Even the marketplace, which was always full of people buying and selling, was deserted.

"Where could all the people be?" he thought.

As Telemachus made his way to the centre of the city, he thought he could hear voices – or was it shouting? As he got closer, the noise was deafening. He arrived at the Colosseum. There were literally thousands upon thousands of people inside.

Well, Telemachus looked into the arena and there, cheered on by thousands of people, were two gladiators with swords. You see, the things that Roman gladiators did were very different to the type of things we might see on the television game show. They were real fighters, and these were fights to the death. Two men would stand in the middle of the arena and would fight with swords until one of them was killed.

As Telemachus watched, the gladiators started to fight. Telemachus couldn't believe what he was seeing as they struck each other again and again until eventually one fell down dead. Telemachus began pushing his way through the crowd to the centre of the arena. Before he could get there, two more gladiators had begun to fight.

As Telemachus got to the centre of the arena, another gladiator fell to the ground, dead.

Telemachus looked up at the Roman emperor Honorius, who was in his royal box enjoying the fighting. Telemachus yelled: "This is not right! It must stop." The crowd fell silent; you could have heard a pin drop. The emperor stood and looked down at Telemachus. Telemachus lifted his voice and said again and again: "This is not right. It must stop."

The emperor lifted his hand, pointed to Telemachus and said, "Kill him!"

To the horror of the crowd, the remaining gladiator walked towards the monk and plunged his sword into his stomach. Telemachus fell, and with his dying breath whispered: "This is not right. This must stop."

Telemachus died, but as he lay on the ground, blood pouring from him, people began to stand and make their way out of the arena until only the emperor sat there. He too stood and left. That was the last ever gladiator fight to take place in the Colosseum.

Telemachus is a hero. Why? Because a hero is someone who stands up for what is right, no matter what the cost.

Crow Starts School

Fox, Rooster, Snake, and Poodle were the best of friends.

Every morning, Rooster would wake up all the animals up with a loud cock-a-doodle-do. They would stretch, ruffle, shake, and then they'd have some breakfast. Rooster would have some corn, Poodle would have a bone, Fox would have some cereal, and Snake would have some spaghetti. They would then set off to the barn where they would have school. Fox, who was a bit older than the others and by far the cleverest of all the animals, taught them. After school, they would all play together before going to their homes to wash, clean their teeth, and go to bed.

Everything was nice in the farmyard, everyone got on with everyone else. They really were the best of friends.

One day, Crow flew into the farmyard and decided he would like to stay there. He went to find Fox to see if he could join in with everyone else and go to school with the other animals. Fox was delighted that Crow wanted to join everyone else. So the very next day, Fox stood at the front of the class and announced that Crow had just arrived and wanted to be friends. So, could everyone make him feel at home?

Crow had a nice day in school and got to meet Rooster, Snake, and Poodle. After school, Crow went to Rooster's house. He knocked on the door and asked if Rooster would come out to play. Well, the weather was nice and it was still quite light so his mother allowed him out to play. They had a great time together. Rooster showed Crow how to go cock-a-doodle-do, and although Crow couldn't quite do it properly, he had fun. But when Rooster went home, Crow went to the other animals and said, "Doesn't Rooster look silly? He's got that really funny thing on his head. It looks like a big red rubber glove."

Fox told Crow that he shouldn't say unkind things, but Crow wouldn't listen.

The next day after school, Crow went to see if Rooster would come out to play, but this time he wouldn't come out. "You said unkind things about me," said Rooster, "and so I'm not going to be your friend anymore."

So Crow went to Snake's house. He knocked on the door and asked if Snake would come out to play. Well, the weather was nice and it was still quite light so his mother allowed him out to play. They had a great time together. Snake showed Crow how to wriggle on his tummy, and although Crow couldn't quite do it properly, he had fun. But when Snake went home, Crow went to the other animals and said, "Doesn't Snake crawl funny? He just wriggles on his tummy getting dust up his nose. He's not very fast and he's hopeless at games."

Fox told Crow that he shouldn't say unkind things but Crow wouldn't listen.

The next day after school, Crow went to see if Snake would come out to play, but this time he wouldn't come out. "You said unkind things about me," said Snake, "and so I'm not going to be your friend anymore."

So Crow went to Poodle's house. He knocked on the door and asked if Poodle would come out to play. Well, the weather was nice and it was still quite light so her mother allowed her out to play. They had a great time together. Poodle showed Crow how to bark and to chase butterflies, and although Crow couldn't quite do it properly, he had fun. But when Poodle went home, Crow went to the other animals and said, "Isn't Poodle silly? She's not very clever at all, is she? She just barks and chases butterflies. She's a little bit stupid, isn't she?"

Fox told Crow that he shouldn't say unkind things but Crow wouldn't listen.

The next day after school, Crow went to see if Poodle would come out to play, but this time she wouldn't come out. "You said unkind things about me," said Poodle, "and so I'm not going to be your friend anymore."

So now Crow had no friends at all. Rooster wouldn't play with him because Crow had said he had a big red rubber glove on his head. Snake wouldn't play with him because Crow had said he couldn't move very fast and was hopeless at games, and Poodle wouldn't play with him because Crow had said she was stupid.

Crow had no friends at all. He was very sad. He was very miserable. He went to see Fox. "What am I to do? I've got no friends and I feel very lonely."

Fox said to Crow, "It's because you were unkind. You must go to each of the animals in turn and apologize and promise never to do it again."

So Crow went to Rooster and said, "I'm sorry I said you had a red rubber glove on your head. I'll never be unkind to you again. Will you forgive me?"

Rooster was kind and forgave Crow.

Crow went to Snake and said, "I'm sorry I said you weren't very good at games. I'll never be unkind again. Will you forgive me?"

Snake was kind and forgave Crow.

Crow went to Poodle and said, "I'm sorry I said you weren't very clever. I'll never be unkind again. Will you forgive me?"

Poodle was very kind and forgave Crow.

So Crow was once again friends with Rooster, Snake and Poodle. All thanks to a very wise animal indeed called Fox.

The Legend of Teddy Stollard

It was the very first day of the new term and everyone was pushing and shoving to be the first into the new classroom. This was a Year 6 class, and they thought if they could get in first then they could have the best seats. Eventually they were all inside and sat down. In walked Mrs Wilson. She stood at the front of the class and said, "OK, Year 6. I want you to know something. In my class there will be no favourites. I will treat everyone exactly the same. Is that clear?"

This was quite a tough Year 6 class, but they were just a little bit frightened of Mrs Wilson, so they nodded and said, "Yes, Miss."

Mrs Wilson was true to her word. She really had no favourites. She treated Robin the same as she treated Jacob, and Alex the same as she treated Stephanie. She treated everyone exactly the same. Well, nearly everyone. You see, there was one little boy named Teddy Stollard who was the rudest, the most obnoxious, the most irritable and horrible boy you could ever hope to meet. When Mrs Wilson asked everyone to stand, he would sit. When she asked everyone to stand in line, he would step out. When she asked everyone to be quiet, he would talk. When she asked everyone to sit down, he would stand on his desk. He really was the most rude, obnoxious, irritable, and horrible boy. And Mrs Wilson really didn't like him much at all – even though she tried to hide it.

The rest of the class didn't like Teddy much either. Not because he was rude, obnoxious, irritable, and horrible, but for something they thought was much worse. Teddy was smelly! He wasn't just a little bit smelly, he was absolutely gross. You could smell him from across the street.

There was a reason why Teddy was smelly. Actually, there were two reasons. The first was simply that he never washed. His hair would stick up in the air, not with gel but with grease. His face and hands were grimy and muddy. His neck was black and he never ever washed under his armpits.

The second reason why Teddy smelt was that he never changed his clothes. His jeans were covered in oil and mud and grass stains and had rips all over. His T-shirt used to be white, but now you could see what Teddy had eaten for the last two months. It had baked bean juice in the corner and tomato ketchup down the front and curry sauce in the middle and Coke splattered everywhere. He never ever changed his socks. Well, he did once and they were so bad he could stick them to the wall. As you can imagine, nobody wanted to be his friend. He would spend lots of time in the playground by himself.

And this was made worse by the fact that he had a game which he loved to play. He would sit in the classroom playing his game. The other children hated his game and they never would have dreamt of playing it. You see, Teddy's favourite game was called Flick the Bogey. He would sit at the back of the class picking his nose and flicking the bogey around the room. He was good at it; he could hit the blackboard from the back of the classroom. Everyone else in the class would play a different sort of game, a game called Dodge the Bogey. Mrs Wilson got lots and lots of letters from parents, complaining. But what was she to do? He just never listened.

Teddy didn't have any friends; let's face it, would you have been his friend?

It came to Christmas-time and it was a bit of a tradition that at Christmas everyone would bring in presents for their teacher. So that's what they did. There were presents wrapped in gold wrapping paper and presents wrapped in Father Christmas paper and presents wrapped in green and red stripy paper. There really were all sorts of presents. And there, lying at the bottom of the pile, was a present wrapped in a brown paper bag. And that present was from…

Mrs Wilson pushed that present away. She was a little bit worried about what she would find inside. She opened a gold-wrapped present, a lovely pair of gloves; she opened a stripy paper present, a new ruler; she opened others and found a scarf, a new pencil case, a new globe. And then after she had opened all the rest she came to the final present. The one wrapped in the brown paper bag.

She took the corners and carefully let the contents fall onto the desk. She looked down and she couldn't believe her eyes. There was a bottle of perfume and a bracelet. But when she looked closer, she could see that the perfume was nearly empty and the bracelet was beginning to rust.

All the children in the class started to laugh and bang on the desks, chanting: "Teddy's smelly, Teddy's smelly."

Teddy didn't know what to do. He could feel his eyes stinging as he tried to hold back the tears. He'd brought in the best presents he could. The class kept chanting, "Teddy's smelly, Teddy's smelly."

Teddy slid down in his chair so that he was nearly under the desk. His eyes couldn't hold back the tears any longer and they ran down his face. Mrs Wilson knew she had to do something, so she grabbed the perfume and sprayed some on. "Isn't that lovely, boys and girls?" she asked.

They all thought, "No, Miss. It's horrible!" But they all replied, "Yes, Miss."

Mrs Wilson then put the bracelet on and said, "Isn't that lovely, boys and girls?"

They all thought, "No, Miss. It's horrible!" But they all replied, "Yes, Miss."

Mrs Wilson then stood up and announced: "Because you've been so kind and brought me all these presents, you may go home early."

So they all made their way out until only two people were left in the classroom – Mrs Wilson and Teddy. Teddy walked up to Mrs Wilson and said, "Mrs Wilson, thank you for wearing that bracelet and putting on the perfume. When you did that, it reminded me so much of my mother."

And with that, he turned and walked out of the room. Mrs Wilson was now seriously confused. She really didn't know what was going on. She went to the cupboard and pulled out Teddy's reports from when he was in Year 3. And she began to read.

Year 3

Teddy is a very clever boy. He does well in class. His appearance is always neat and tidy.

Mrs Thompson thought she was reading the wrong report. She checked the file again. It was definitely his.

Year 4

Teddy is a very clever boy. He does well in class. His appearance is always neat and tidy.

And then, at the very bottom in the section called "Comments", it said this: *Teddy is finding it increasingly hard to concentrate right now as his mother is really ill.*

Year 5

Teddy's work has gone from bad to worse. His appearance has gone from bad to worse. His attitude has gone from bad to worse. He's becoming rude and obnoxious. And he's beginning to smell.

Then, in brackets at the bottom of the page, in the "Comments" section, it said these words: *Teddy's mother died this year.*

And here he was in Year 6. Yes, he was smelly, but that was because his mother had died and his father was so upset that he would spend every evening crying and not looking after Teddy. Teddy was so upset that he had started being rude and nasty.

Mrs Wilson knew that she had to help. So she got special people to help Teddy's dad. And she began to give Teddy extra lessons. Before long, his dad began to cope better and Teddy began to improve. By the end of Year 6, he was right back at the top of the class. And off Teddy went to secondary school.

A year later, Mrs Wilson found a note under her door from Teddy, telling her that of all the teachers he'd had in junior school, she was his favourite. Six years went by before she got another note from Teddy. And then he wrote that he had finished secondary school third in his class, and she was still his favourite teacher of all time. Four years after that she got another letter, saying that while things had been tough at times, he'd stayed in school, had stuck with it, and would be leaving university with the highest of honours. He assured Mrs Wilson she was still his favourite teacher.

The story doesn't end there. You see, there was yet another letter that spring. Teddy said that he'd met a lovely girl and was to be married, and he was wondering if Mrs Wilson might agree to sit in the pew usually reserved for the mother of the groom. So Mrs Wilson went to the wedding, and Teddy had his favourite teacher there.